CW01456136

who will be remembered here

who will be remembered here

Queer Spaces in Scotland

A collection conceived and curated by
Lewis Hetherington and CJ Mahony

HISTORIC ENVIRONMENT SCOTLAND

ÀRAINNEACHD EACHDRAIDHEIL ALBA

Published in 2025 by
Historic Environment Scotland Enterprises Limited SC510997

HISTORIC ENVIRONMENT SCOTLAND | ÀRAINNEACHD EACHDRAIDHEIL ALBA

Historic Environment Scotland
Longmore House
Salisbury Place
Edinburgh EH9 1SH

Registered Charity SC045925

British Library Cataloguing-in-Publication Data.
A catalogue record for this book is available from the British Library.

ISBN 978 1 84917 369 8

Individual stories remain copyright of their respective authors
The Library is a Queer Thing © Mae Diansangu, 2025
The Strathclyde Suite © Damian Barr, 2025
Red Blaes and Blue Moon © Amanda Thomson, 2025
Sm:)e for 2004 / Sm:)e airson 2004 © MJ Deans, 2025
A Subtractive Process © CJ Mahony, 2025
My Sapphic City © Ashley Douglas, 2025
The Club, 4 Queens Crescent © Louise Welsh, 2025
20-Something Spittal Street © Ink Asher Hemp, 2025
Little Gless Box © Johnny McKnight, 2025
Nowhere © Ali Smith, 2025
Glasgow's Queer Foundations © Jeff Meek, 2025
Earth Inferno © Ever Dundas, 2025
Mary's Cottage © Lewis Hetherington, 2025
Piper's Cave © Rona Munro, 2025

© Historic Environment Scotland 2025

All rights reserved. No part of this publication may be reproduced, stored in or introduced into a retrieval system, or transmitted, in any form, or by any means (electronic, mechanical, photocopying, recording or otherwise) without the prior written permission of Historic Environment Scotland.

Typeset in Optima, Garamond and Gotham

Printed in the UK by Clays Ltd, Elcograf S.p.A.

MIX
Paper | Supporting responsible forestry
FSC® C018072
www.fsc.org

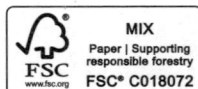

Contents

Introduction

Queerness threads and weaves through every part of Scottish history, but it is largely intangible. Records are not kept or are deliberately destroyed. Very few places or buildings belong specifically to our community as evidence of the queer lives that have come before. By making these invisible stories visible, *who will be remembered here* captures something of the richness, complexity and beauty of this shared queer history.

At the root of *who will be remembered here* are questions about which stories we, as a society, choose to tell, and how these stories shape the lives of later generations. In this collection, we wanted to look at history through a queer lens, to find kinship with those whose stories could so easily be lost. This perspective illuminated the many marginalised and oppressed voices which have been disappeared from the historical record. This book is a cry against the erasure of cultures, languages and identities which has defined our past, and which threatens to define our futures.

Our contributors were invited to share stories of places in Scotland that are part of their history, especially places that are not always considered historically significant. We worked with authors who write from distinct perspectives, who write in different languages, whose autobiographies inform their work in diverse ways. These writers offer us a chance to reconsider and reimagine the history of our built and natural environment through a personal lens, finding value and significance where it is often unseen. They offer us stories which are tender, funny, thought-provoking and begin to gesture at the multiplicity of experience that exists in our shared history.

who will be remembered here is an archive for the future.

At a time when forceful movements in our society wish to deny the existence and validity of certain lives, we seek to document and celebrate queer bodies and the intersection of their identities and experiences. We want to populate Scotland's collective cultural memory with the full spectrum of people who have lived here in the past, and those who will come to live here in the future.

Lewis and CJ
June 2025

who will be remembered here

Woodside Library

The Library is a
Queer Thing

MAE DIANSANGU

How strange to find an unselfish building that doesn't ask anything of us. Many of our public buildings only know how to love conditionally: *you can stay here for as long as you're paying.* The Library proudly others itself when it chooses to give more than it takes. The Library is a queer thing. It exists in spaces of transition and potential. Constantly in flux – books, ideas and people move through it – reshaping its purpose and meaning with every inter- action. The Library is a refuge where exploration and questioning are encouraged, which is perhaps the queerest thing of all.

I want to tell you about My First Library. It was a gift to the people of Woodside, Aberdeen, dating back to the 1880s. Sir John Anderson wanted to honour the commu- nity that raised him, so he gave them The Library. Like all good gifts it was freely given, with no expectation of return. More than a hundred years later, I opened that gift.

I want to tell you about Woodside Library, how it felt to find myself inside it. Stepping onto the burgundy carpet that greeted each patron as a distinguished guest, I knew that I was welcome. The warmth from this reception, and the great cast-iron radiators I would lean against for support, generated the cosiest of feelings.

I want to tell you about Woodside Library, but really I am talking about All Libraries. Each library contains the essence of the whole, to step into one is to step into all of them. All Libraries are connected in a way that transcends the physical. A shining network of knowledge, bound by hope, imagination and curiosity. All Libraries are reflections of one another in an expansive ecosystem that supports their shared mission: to provide stories and communities with room to grow together.

My First Library
My dog is smart, but not book smart. She is in fact illiterate. Still, I point out My First Library to her. How its door sighs under the weight of a council-sanctioned padlock. I entertain the idea that animals can feel the past more keenly than us. When my dog's ears prick up, I wonder if she hears my footsteps from several shoe sizes ago, running up to a door not yet slammed shut.

Growing up is hard to do. I know it isn't easy for anyone, but my younger self saw people gliding, skipping, laughing through it. Seemingly, everyone around me knew what to say and how to say it. They knew how to play, how to regulate their emotions, how to look like other people, how to navigate their body. I watched them, and I watched myself watching them. This was a clever trick I learned from feeling disconnected; I could leave my body to get a bird's-eye view. This was especially helpful when I needed to judge myself extra harshly or compare myself to others who were a lot better at being Normal. I was not Normal. The ever-present feeling that I was *wrong* and *different* announced this. Adult me would one day learn about neurodivergence and queerness and the impact racism has on mental health; little me just felt at odds with myself and my surroundings.

I don't remember the first time I entered Woodside Library, in the same way I don't remember the first time I met my grandparents. Simply, it had always been there. Always close by, always familiar. Fitting, as John Anderson explicitly gifted The Library to the people of Woodside *in perpetuity*. Sturdy and dependable, The Library became my safe space. It wasn't like school with its noisy demands. There was no pressure to perform or fit in. The burden of figuring out people's expectations, and the anxiety that I would fail them, was removed completely. Just to move through the quiet space – browsing, flicking pages, picking up books and putting them back down – was calming. The act of choosing a book became sacred. It felt private and special; a choice that the adults had trusted me to make for myself. At home, space – and consequently privacy – were at a premium. The Library offered room to walk off the growing pains. It allowed me to take something that was just for me. I was grateful for its expansive windows that framed clouds and treetops. The panes of glass were strategically placed high enough so that only the sky could look in on what you were doing. This was the magic of The Library – private moments unfolding in a public space. It was the perfect way to find solitude within community. Alone, but not lonely. I could be my quiet weirdo self out in the open, and that was completely acceptable.

You Are What You Read
Library books are a different breed. They are more patient than other books because The Library encourages you to take as much time as you need. As a child, I could feel this in The Library's gentle sounds: the pleasant thunk of books landing on the return trolley; an occasional flutter of pages; hushed voices that respected the stillness of

hallowed spaces. A soft silence that whispered, 'There's no rush here.' The right book was always happy to wait for me, and when I was ready, it would make my acquaintance. The Library knew I was queer before I did. Why else would it so lovingly nudge me into stories that spoke to the subconscious parts of myself? I say stories, but really they were mirrors and doorways. The long shadow cast by Section 28 obscured many paths I might have walked to self-discovery. But The Library was there, dropping hints. I didn't need to ask, *what is it about **this** book and **these** characters that makes me feel reassured and comforted?* I accepted the books as they were, gathering clues without realising.

When I was twelve, The Library introduced me to a book that would prove to be formative. It was written by a queer person. At the time, I didn't know the author was queer, and I certainly didn't know that about myself either. But I *did* know we had something important in common: we were both Black and Scottish. Before *Straw Girl* by Jackie Kay found me, I hadn't met a character whose racial and national identities aligned so closely with mine. As I turned the pages, the transformation took place. I wasn't just a reader anymore; I became part of the narrative. It felt as if I moved from outside the book to inside it. This shift was so powerful. It felt like I could exist in multiple places; in this way, to simultaneously be a reader and to be read was like defying physics, defying limitations. I was no longer on the outside, observing. I was allowed to *belong*.

The Library made this experience possible. Without its kind shelves steering me towards myself, how long would I have had to wait to discover *Straw Girl*? How long would it have taken for me to see myself reflected in a story? Encountering Jackie Kay's writing in childhood unknowingly initiated a lifelong relationship with Black queerness

– in literature and within myself. It doesn't matter that I learned about her queerness years later. What matters is that I was exposed to a Black queer voice when I wasn't aware such a thing existed.

Some years after losing/finding myself in *Straw Girl*, I would read Jackie Kay's *Trumpet* (another library book) at a time when I couldn't yet acknowledge my own queerness. The novel, with its Black, queer central character, would resonate with me in ways I couldn't fully understand. I would revisit it later, when my identity made more sense to me. Like many queer people, I didn't have a single coming-out moment or an epiphany; it was more like an unravelling. The Library gifting me Kay's work early on was so meaningful – it created a connection I could return to. By the time I revisited *Trumpet* with a better understanding of my queerness, it felt like coming out to an old friend. A friend who had more tact than to boast 'Ha! I knew it!', but instead put the kettle on and said, 'Welcome home'.

There were other books that would jump off The Library's shelves when they saw me coming – books whose authors I would later find out were queer. Jacqueline Wilson and Ann M Martin made a significant contribution to my personal archive of identity. The girls in their stories fascinated me. Martin's much beloved *Baby-sitters Club* series followed a group of precocious young girls who Got Stuff Done. Each story was narrated by a different member of this group of besties. Whoever the narrator was, they always made sure to let the reader know – yes, they were all different, but their friendship was founded on respect for, and appreciation of these differences. Wilson's girls were often marginalised, but remained resilient, bright, funny, curious, defiant and brave. I loved how messy their lives could feel.

A new layer of meaning emerged when I learned these authors were queer. I could see how deeply aspects of my identity had always been entwined with the stories I loved. These books subtly demonstrated that queerness could exist in ordinary lives, in everyday struggles and triumphs, even when it wasn't explicitly named. They spoke about community, chosen family and taking pride in difference. The characters dealt with the mucky feelings brought about by the trauma of being *other*, but were ultimately able to be their authentic selves.

Revisiting and rediscovering queer writers is a huge comfort to both versions of myself, past and present. I still return to the books of my childhood to reconnect with my younger self – to acknowledge them, to reassure them, and to recognise and honour an identity rooted in queerness that was there all along. For many queer people, to remember the past is to reshape it. We look back, not just to see things as they were, but to imagine how they might have been.

The Library's Guide to Building Yourself

I often don't feel comfortable visiting The Past. It hasn't always done a great job of making me feel welcome or creating space for me. I am, however, physically very close to it. My dog and I walk past My First Library three or four times a week. Its neighbouring building, now called Omega Fire Ministries, was known as the Burgh Hall when I took dance lessons there. Right across the road stands my old primary school. So much of my childhood was spent moving between these three solid Victorian buildings, I like to think their granite walls absorbed my memories to keep them safe. The day after I decide to write about The Library, I take the ten-minute trip from my house to loosen some memories from the stone. While my dog reads the invisible scent trails lingering on the pavement, I press my palm against the wall surrounding the building. Cold spreads through my hand, and from this damp feeling, a memory seeps out: the great summer reading challenge of '99.

It was all fairly straightforward. Check a book out, read it. Write a wee summary detailing your favourite part and how the book made you feel. Then show the librarian, who would give a quick glance over what you had written and stamp a card to record how much you had read. Leave it to The Library to think of a way to make reading even more exciting and addictive. The thrill of competing with myself to read as much as possible mixed with the validation that came with every stamp was a heady cocktail indeed. Perhaps the most exciting part of all was the folder each participant of the challenge was given to keep all the reports together. I kept this folder for years. I never questioned why I was so attached to it, but now I see it for the brilliant gift it was – a personal archive capturing the influences that shaped me.

Tucking each finished report into the folder and revisiting them later became a cherished ritual. Today, I have apps like StoryGraph and Letterboxd to record the books and films I've enjoyed, but the essence remains the same: creating a personal catalogue has always held deep meaning for me. I think the summer reading challenge was the first time I really engaged in this process. What began as a simple hyperfixation to occupy a weird eight year old built the foundations of a love for archiving the experiences and influences that make me who I am.

In 1999, I couldn't tell you why keeping a reading record was so much fun. Now I understand the process of cataloguing books as a way to articulate who I am. When I looked through my folder, I accessed the memories linked to each individual book. What else was happening in my life when I read them? What stories captured my attention at that time? All of this mapped the evolution of my tastes. It was a visual representation of how stories could shape a person and help construct identity. *You are what you read*. It was a way to preserve tangible evidence of internal transformations – the imprint of each story on my life.

As a queer adult, I see the importance of keeping personal records. For queer people, creating and preserving personal archives often takes on a political dimension. It becomes an act of resistance – fighting against erasure, conformity and invisibility. Personal archives can offer some of the most authentic insights into queer life, especially when history is riddled with gaps and silences. They serve as a way to document lives and stories that might otherwise be forgotten.

For much of my life, I was oblivious to queerness because it wasn't part of the fabric of my reality or the society around me. Queer histories and realities, myths and legends, were suppressed or ignored, and as a result, they couldn't reach me. A personal archive doesn't exist solely for the individual – it also serves as a bridge to others. Sharing a favourite queer novel, a playlist of queer artists, or even a journal entry, can foster solidarity and understanding. Every individual archive, though deeply personal, contributes to the broader tapestry of queer history, forming a collective narrative of resilience, creativity and transformation.

The day after I decide to write about The Library, the bell from my old primary school rings to let the children know it's playtime. It pulls me out of the memory from twenty-five summers ago and I am struck by the feeling that these buildings still have the power to move me.

Another feeling emerges: as I reach into the past, I am also stretching forward, yet somehow my hands meet. I realise I am caught in a web of time, where the task of remembering isn't as straightforward as looking straight behind you. I realise that maybe time isn't straight after all.

The Library Runs on Queer Time

In The Library, time bends and folds in on itself. For me, the feeling that time moves differently in this space has always been palpable – the way I could lose hours yet gain infinite possibilities. The Library can reveal a book that will suddenly transport you to a different era, a different life, a different word of potential. Past, present and future coexist within its walls. This is not dissimilar to how I experience queerness – feeling like I exist in overlapping timelines.

There's the timeline where I navigate life without fully understanding I'm queer. This timeline is marked by fairly typical events. Things like going to school; getting a library card; learning to ride a bike; experiencing heartbreak for the first time (the absolute worst anyone has ever felt in recorded history, by the way); eventually becoming someone who can earnestly say *I am not a virgin*, but still doesn't really understand what all the fuss is about; going to university and realising I've apparently been using 'made-up' words my whole life (see *chipper, softie, bosie).*

Then there is the timeline where I have fully embodied my queerness and get to experience 'firsts' as this person. Quieter milestones, like re-reading *Trumpet,* feel small and private in a way that doesn't diminish their power. Loud moments, like orgasms, reconfigure past notions of the body and its limitations. As these timelines intersect each other, queer life doesn't feel like it moves forward in a neat, linear progression.

'Queer time' is very much a thing. So says queer theorist and academic Jack Halberstam, who argues that queer uses of time 'develop, at least in part, in opposition to the institutions of family, heterosexuality, and reproduction'. Following this, queer subcultures 'produce alternative temporalities by allowing their participants to believe that their futures can be imagined according to logics that lie outside of those paradigmatic markers of life experience – namely, birth, marriage, reproduction, and death'.[1]

Halberstam says that queer lives often tick outside the heteronormative clock. There is no shortage of messages from society telling us what the hour should be, according to straight time, but where do we find alternative views so we can imagine futures that don't align with this clock? Without knowing the significance of this gift, The Library was the first place that offered me a space where the markers of heteronormative temporality could be challenged. I was often drawn to books where traditional family conventions were disrupted (Jacqueline Wilson being a prime example of this). I jumped headfirst into the stories where characters forged their own paths, reaching their goals in unexpected and unconventional ways. These stories may not have been explicitly queer, but they resisted societal timelines.

If queer people process time in ways that challenge traditional constructions, then The Library becomes an ideal space to learn how to disrupt these norms. The Library built a path for me to inhabit queer temporality, suggesting that there is no singular truth or fixed trajectory. Instead, it revealed an expansive web of potential timelines and realities, each waiting to be explored. The

1   J Halberstam, *Queer Time and Place: Transgender Bodies, Subcultural Lives*, New York: New York University Press, 2005

Library taught me to play with time, encouraging me to step outside my own chronology into alternative timescapes.

The Library as a Victim of War
When I look at The Library of today, I still see The Library of my childhood – just as I sometimes catch a sliver of my younger self shining behind my much older eyes. Both The Library and I have changed over time. Sometimes together, sometimes apart. The Library was an important companion in transformation – a space of growth, learning and self-discovery. Now, having returned to the area where I grew up, I still feel the bond we shared, but I also see the changes in both of us. This shared history makes me feel that our journeys will always be intertwined, yet I can't help but sense that the evolution and progress we've made may be under threat.

The Library is an endangered species. In May 2023, Woodside Library closed its doors forever. Aberdeen City Council's decision was fought the entire way, but despite community outrage the local authority culled a total of six libraries at this time. I am writing this about 18 months since these closures, and about two weeks since it was announced that Aberdeenshire is set to lose thirteen libraries. Those who campaigned to save their beloved public buildings are still looking for answers. Hayden Lorimer, Woodside resident and library campaigner, laments the persistent lack of transparency regarding the closures:

> *I submitted a freedom of information request. I wanted to learn more about the legal advice that had satisfied council officers that historic restrictions placed on the use of our library building by Sir John Anderson … 'were no longer valid or enforceable'. My FOI*

request was turned down. I asked that the decision be reviewed. The panel didn't budge. So, I lodged an appeal with the Scottish Information Commissioner... The Commissioner's judgement deems it appropriate that the council be allowed to obtain comprehensive and candid legal advice in confidence.[2]

If ever there was a building that took candour seriously, it was The Library. The council's refusal to provide clarity around their decision feels like a betrayal of The Library's core ethos: openness, education and accessibility. For decades, The Library has served as a space of transparency and truth-seeking, inviting communities to explore and imagine freely. The way in which those responsible for disappearing The Library are so committed to burying their motives shows a clear disdain for the values the building came to represent.

I refuse to believe The Library was closed because of a lack of money – much more likely it was due to a lack of value placed on meeting the needs of the community. Rather than unavoidable casualties of austerity, library closures feel as intentional as acts of war. I find it difficult to view the war against The Library as distinct from the war against queerness. Both are ideological battles against possibility. In both cases, people are restricted in what they can imagine, explore or become.

The Future

We are living in the age of disinformation and disappearing libraries: a dangerous combination for queer people. In recent years, there has been a marked increase in anti-LGBTQ+ rhetoric, with trans people being singled out

2   H Lorimer, 'Lack of candour behind library closures', *The Press and Journal*, 11 December 2024

for the harshest and most sustained attacks. Particularly in online spaces, there is a disturbing trend of elevating non-experts, which is a primary symptom of anti-intellectualism. (Other symptoms include, but are not limited to: promotion of conspiracy theories; hostility towards academic institutions; rejection of critical thinking; contempt for the arts and humanities.) The future of All Libraries and queer people depends on our commitment to valuing education and access to knowledge.

Growing up, The Library was more to me than just a place to hold books. It was a living, breathing community resource, a space where I could learn, explore and grow. The experiences I had there were foundational, creating connections I could always return to. Inside those walls, I unknowingly laid the groundwork for understanding queerness. For a child that felt different, it offered comfort as a refuge that nurtured both my curiosity and my sense of self. My hope is that future queer generations can discover themselves in a world that cherishes and protects The Library's values. I want The Library of my past to be the The Library of their future – a space of limitless possibilities where they are encouraged to learn, build and explore, in their own time.

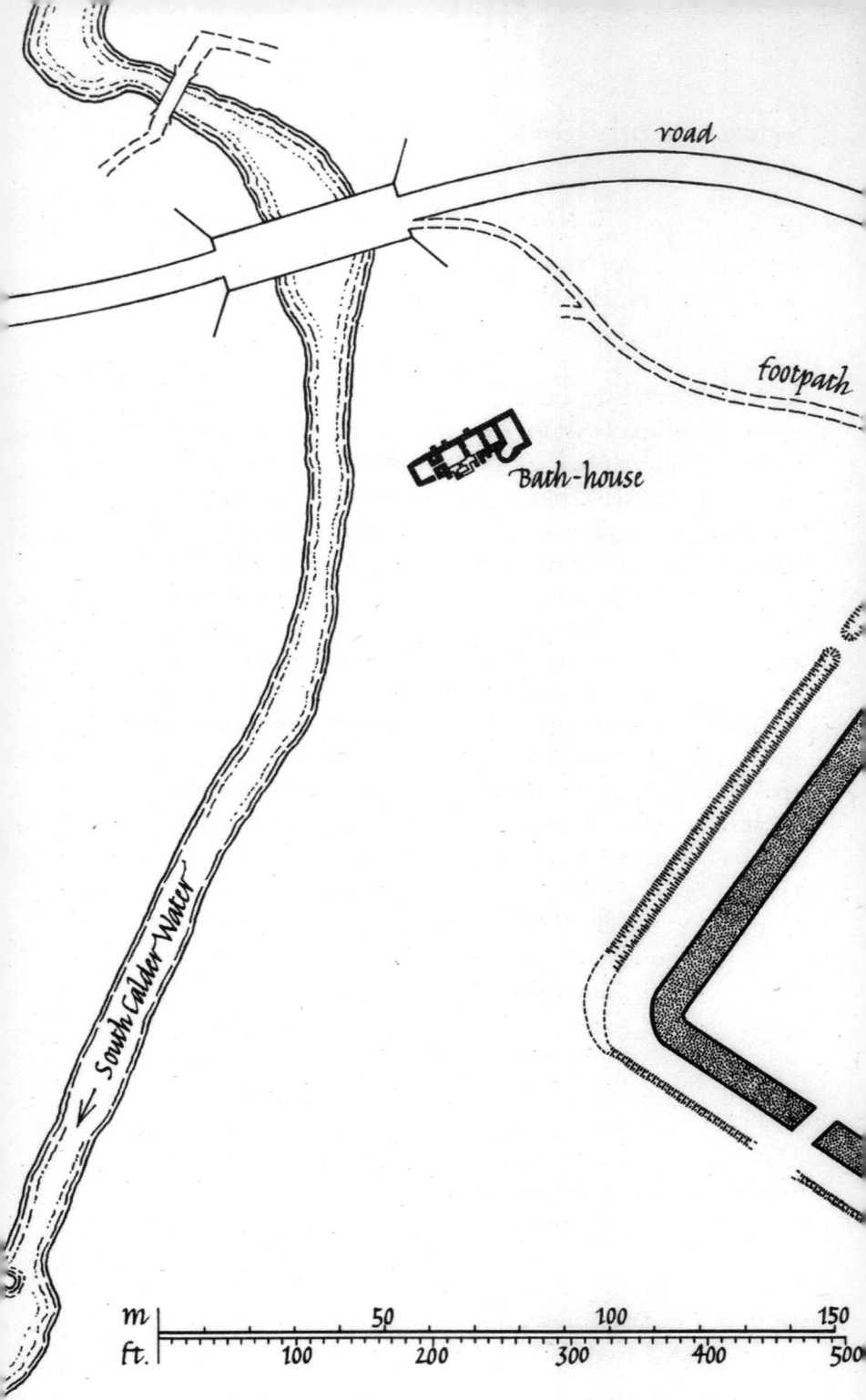

road

footpath

Bath-house

South Calder Water

m		50		100		150
ft.	100	200	300	400	500

The Strathclyde Suite

DAMIAN BARR

The sun has never been brighter than it is today. You wouldn't believe this is Scotland. Light batters off the water in Strathclyde Park – like something out a holiday advert off the telly, like a destination you'd have to pay off every week. The Costa Del Motherwell. The air is sticky with candy floss and a machiney oily smell from the shows, the Wurlitzer whirling, the sound pulling us all in, light bulbs burning even on this July day. The ghost train screams, the rollercoaster rattles, we all want more.

I squint at the shows through the fringe I cut for myself because my Mum and Dad can't agree who's taking me to the barbers since they got their d-i-v-o-r-c-e: they still spell it out when me and my wee sister are about. As if we've not heard it shouted, whispered, cried a million times already. As if I'm not still the best speller in my class.

Today is my birthday treat: I'm eight years old and about to turn nine – soon I'll be in double figures and then I'll be at Brannock High School and away from all the boys that chase me home when the bell rings. But this is not a story about home, although maybe all stories are.

Today, it's just me and my Dad. This never happens. Coins clank in his pockets – columns of copper and silver stacked in his big rough hands.

'Mon, I'll show you how to drive,' he says, flipping a

fifty pence piece into the air so it flashes in the sun like a freshly-caught fish. Are there fish in the water that laps the pebbly beach by the car park? There's leeches, I've heard. What else? Does a distant family member from *The Family Ness* cartoon sleep at the bottom of the loch with the Fine Fayre trolleys? A dinosaur in Motherwell, that would be cool. But no, I think, there's nothing old here – no big houses, no thatch on our roofs, no Tudors or even Stuarts. I've read about history further up the map, in the Highlands and on some of the magic-sounding islands, but not down here. We've not even any ghosts – they only stay in big posh houses. We got our new house (front and back door) after the old lady that lived in it died. I told my Mum I was scared she'd haunt us but she said the council can evict anybody. There's no capital H History round here – the stoor of it can't settle, maybe it's something to do with all the smoke and noise from the Ravenscraig, maybe it's because of all the future made from all the steel made by all the Dads, mine included.

That fifty pence piece, it's still turning in the air.

Heads. Tails. Heads. Tails. My Dad snatches it mid-spin, could catch the whole world in his hands. He nods to me then flicks the coin right at me. I don't reach out for it or even fumble it. I just step back. It lands on the dry summer grass between us and sits there accusing me of something I don't yet understand.

To make this moment go away, I snatch the coin up and offer it back but my Dad points to the dodgems. The music stops and the cars roll to a halt and the seatbelts clank as everybody gets off, shouting and laughing, turning invisible steering wheels with their hands. *Some speed! You're banned! You drive like a maniac!*

'Hurry up, afore they start again,' my Dad says. He

points to a boy standing with one foot on the edge of the ride, like he owns it – he's wearing a blue Nike shell suit I've not seen in any catalogue.

'Pay the boy.'

I stand up straight and walk over and, as I get close, I notice bum fluff on his top lip and a cold sore on the way out. His hair is perfect ginger curtains. He must be a fourth year.

'Two,' I say, holding out the fifty pence so he can see it. I don't say please but would if I was with my Mum.

The boy tugs open a brown leather money belt tied tight round his waist. The mouth of it yawns and I glimpse a hoard glinting in there. I can smell the leather, see millions of tiny dimples in it. He juts one hip out then points at his belt. A queue shuffles behind me. 'Two,' he says, in an accent not from here, then knocks the coin from my hand into his belt, janking in with all the others. Could I still pick it out – would it feel different?

Electric guitar music roars up and a fake American accent says, 'Buckle up folks!' My Dad steps on to the rink which is matt black streaked with grey where the bumpers scuff it. I slip-stagger on the rubber, the same as my gym plimsolls. Somehow, my Dad folds himself into the glittery silver car, the seatbelt barely crossing his chest, his knees up round his chin. I slide in next to him, the black vinyl seat still warm from the people before us. There's just enough room.

My Dad turns to me and grins and suddenly he is eight again, nearly nine: 'You steer.' As his feet find the pedal, sparks crackle where our car's pole touches the wire roof overhead. I reach across him and he doesn't back away and as I put my hands on the clammy wheel he lays his hands over mine and puts his foot down and we're away. I hope the ginger boy is watching.

History is one of many new things about high school, along with writing in pen, the excitement of exams and the possibility of escaping to university at the end. The Romans are one of our first subjects and I'm shocked to discover they bothered to invade Lanarkshire.

So, I pay the 20p for the bus from Newarthill down the brae through Motherwell past the Ravenscraig and on down to Strathclyde Park where, my history teacher says, the Romans left behind a bathhouse. I sit on the 92 and wonder how old this long straight road really is – if I stay on the bus will it eventually get to Rome?

I find the bathhouse just beyond the shows, which are now here all year round. It had always been here, I just never noticed it, was distracted by the dodgems, by the possibility of a paddle. In the school library I learned that the loch wasn't always here – the cold still waters cover an old mining village called Bothwellhaugh which was abandoned then flooded in the early 1970s, not long before I was born. I imagine all the streets and buildings still down there: a Lanarkshire Atlantis. Is there still a church with a tower and bells that ring but only at midnight? A sign marks the Roman ruins and tells me they were discovered when the village was being demolished and that archaeologists raised them up to save them from the water.

I'm the only person here on this nothing November day.

All that's left are the lowest bits of the walls, the outlines of rooms. I lay my arm across a wall – it's thicker than my arm is long. The stone is the same grey as Motherwell Library. I step in and invite the past back. This 'vestibule' gives way to a 'cold room', two 'warm rooms' and then a 'hot room'. The Romans had heating a thousand years before the council put in our gas radiators! The sign says:

'Up to twenty soldiers at a time could have used the bathhouse. In Roman times, bathing was a social occasion, not just for personal hygiene.' I conjure up twenty men right where I am standing, all in bright white togas like from *Clash of the Titans*. They would have been soldiers – the bathhouse was built around the same time as the Antonine Wall, which was the northern frontier of the Roman Empire in AD 142. So, the men would have been strong. They would have had scars. After a day patrolling, they would have stood their swords together in the vestibule and taken off their armour then moved from room to room, getting hotter as they go, their muscles slowly relaxing. Somehow there would have been red grapes on a silver platter and fluttering music. What language would they have spoken? If I heard them now, would I understand them? Would they understand me? I say out loud the only three Latin words I know: *veni vidi vici*. Except we weren't conquered, were we? I'm here because of the people who were here first. The Romans left, didn't they? My ancestors survived.

My words summon a centurion. He stands in the vestibule of the bathhouse. He's younger than my Dad. His beard and hair are the same dark as his eyes, which glitter like the coal from here that made somebody rich but nobody I know. He has dust on his brown leather sandals from faraway places. He leans against what's left of the wall. *Can anybody else see the centurion?* But it's only me here.

Twenty men lounging around right where I'm standing on cold wet stone. My centurion unbuckles his sword, the golden hilt an eagle taking flight. He smiles uncertainly. What became of him then? Did he run away? Did one of my ancestors strike him down? Is he buried here? Do his bones wait deep beneath the shows, shaking as the rollercoaster thunders by? Is his spirit trapped inside the ghost train, shouting in Latin to be freed? If I dig for him will I find him and if I find him will he be grateful?

Apparently, a cup was found here too but it's in a museum in Glasgow now and there's no picture. I imagine it was carved from horn and filled with rich red wine. Less romantic was a circular stone drain cover with six sort-of-petals radiating out from a hole in the middle. It's also somewhere else. There must be other things waiting to be found.

If there were soldiers, there must also have been a fort and the sign confirms the remains of one lie nearby, but the rain is starting and I'd rather stay here, in the imagined warm. I need to get the bus home soon. Tonight, I will do my homework about visiting the bathhouse – about the surviving structure, its advanced technology, its links to the Antonine Wall. I won't mention my centurion.

*

It seems like a great idea to dress up as Alexis Colby from *Dynasty* for the school sponsored walk around the water in Strathclyde Park. I'll definitely be the only Alexis. It's four miles from start to finish, or about a hundred miles in your Mum's high heels. I'm walking in aid of Oxfam on account of the famines on the news. I curse the children then feel guilty as I force my feet into the shoes I lifted from my Mum's wardrobe this morning. I'm 14 and already hitting six foot so don't really need them and can't believe how wee my Mum's feet are. I squash the backs of the heels down and this works – until I need to stand up. I stagger against the wall of the toilet cubicle where I'm getting changed before our whole year heads down to Strathy.

My dress is actually the two-piece suit in black lace that my Mum saves for funerals. I step into the skirt, the inside is silky-slidy but my big toe snags on the lace. I didn't think to take some tights. The jacket has three fabric-covered buttons and barely goes across my chest, it's halfway up my arms but in a way I think could look quite *Dynasty*. I pull the cubicle door towards me and squeeze past, hobbling out to the sink to do my makeup. I've borrowed lipstick, mascara and something called a pan stick. The lipstick pinks my very buck teeth and I lick them clean, it tastes waxy and secret. I give up on the mascara immediately because I feel sure I'll blind myself. The pan stick hides my spots, just, and I feel a newfound respect for the girls in the year above.

I've told nobody about my costume. I filled my sponsor form with £20 by only going to the doors of the new bought houses built where the Bing used to be and where I played as a boy, before my parents divorced. The Bing was a mini-mountain rising between New Stevenston and Newarthill. It was glittering black diamonds of old coal and slag, shifting cliffs taken over by flaming pink spires of rosebay willowherb. There was a big wild pond filled with cars and couches and somehow frogs which would swim into the white plastic of old fridges, making them easy to see and catch. Where do the frogs go now? Do they turn up at the bright white plastic doors of the new houses?

My make-up is done. My outfit is on. I'm ready. I know I'll get slagged for this and maybe worse. But I'll get slagged anyway. Something about the Strathy makes it okay for me to go as Alexis Colby – I would never walk down my own street like this. But the shows make Strathy less real, more sensational, more glamorous. People go there to feel different. It is a place outside of the everyday.

I have always understood this. I remember the boy who took the money for the dodgems and wonder if he'd recognise me like this, then realise I could never run in these shoes.

*

It's just a car park in a corner of Strathy but it's also nearly midnight and none of us are allowed to be here. It's the end of our final summer holidays and the sky is still a wee bit light in the highest parts. I'm in the backseat with My Mark, who I've known since I was ten and who has also just turned seventeen. Sitting in the front is Other Mark, whose tanned face is framed by natural curls and who looks like he could be in East 17 – he's My Mark's boyfriend, we still giggle when we say the word and only ever say it out loud to each other. Our driver is David, who went to school with Other Mark and who clearly fancies My Mark as well. Nobody is interested in me but it's too exciting to think about that right now.

We all know each other because My Mark rang a phone number that was felt-tipped on the door of the men's toilets in the new McDonalds in Motherwell. A guy answered and they met up but nothing happened and through him we met Other Mark and David, whose parents bought him this car for his 18th. We're all well under the age of consent – 21 is a lifetime away. The Marks haven't waited, I've heard all about it, made My Mark promise to get a condom and use it.

'So, is this the place?' I ask, poking my head between the two front seats as the car engine ticks.

'Aye,' says David, flicking our headlights off. 'We just have to wait.'

'For what?' My Mark asks.

'For that,' says Other Mark as another car swings in behind us, the headlights scouring the car park's corners and briefly lighting us all up. I cover my face instinctively. Everybody laughs.

'What now?' I ask.

David clicks the stereo on and it glows red and orange. Clyde 1 is playing late-night love songs. We all groan and pretend to be sick so he clicks it off again.

This must be near where my Dad parked that time he brought me to Strathy for my birthday. I look out at the trees, their outline dark against the never-black summer sky. They're bigger now. So am I.

'So, people really come here and …?' I let the sentence hang.

Other Mark kids on that he's unzipping his jeans and bucks his hips in the air. We all laugh.

'But …' I persist, not quite sure how to say it. 'Guys … men?'

David checks the other car in his rearview mirror then turns to me.

'Aye, guys … men.'

Another car turns in and it's white and we worry it's the police but it's got no blue light.

'You should go and chap on the windae,' says My Mark to me.

'That's not how it works,' says David. 'They pull up next to you and you look over and they look back.'

'You don't get out,' says Other Mark. 'Only if you're going in the bushes wi somebody.'

The bushes around the car park tremble. I think of Birnam Wood coming to Dunsinane. Anybody could be out there. Did the centurions use these trees for cover – were there even trees here in Roman times? You see boys on the news that go missing and something in their eyes tells me why they went out, what they were hoping to find. I don't want to end up like them.

'Swap seats?' says Other Mark. I shrug. My Mark nods. There is a confusion of legs and arms and a handbrake nearly going where it shouldn't as he clambers into the back and I fall into the front. I click my seatbelt on automatically then take it off slowly as if everybody hasn't already seen. The Marks kiss audibly. David smiles over at me awkwardly.

Suddenly our car lights up – headlights flash on behind us. On then off. On then off. It can't be an accident. *Heads. Tails. Heads. Tails.* My Dad would kill me if he knew where I was.

'It's a new Ford,' says David, checking his mirror. 'Nice car.'

'You would go with somebody because of their car?' I ask.

'No,' he squirms. 'But it's a good start.'

The Marks aren't bothered. They've got each other.

'Should we flash back?' I ask.

'We'd have to turn round,' says David, his hands hovering over the steering wheel.

'Or….' says My Mark, freeing his lips for a moment. 'Yous two could just?'

David shakes his head too fast then says: 'No offence.'

'None taken,' I say, even though that's not exactly how I feel.

I fill the frigid pause: 'So how did you find this place? It's not on the map.'

He thinks for a moment then turns to me and takes a deep breath. 'A guy brought me here once. Then he dropped me off back near my house. I just memorised the road.'

I don't ask about the guy. We all have a guy. 'I wonder

how he found it?'

David shrugs.

How does anybody find anywhere? How did my centurion end up here? At the end of the longest road from Rome.

The clock on the dashboard is now well past midnight. I push myself back in the seat, as if I'm on the dodgems again. I close my eyes and think about the village at the bottom of the water. I imagine silver fish swimming along the submerged streets, in and out of windows and doors, how they shimmer with delight when the bells in the church tower ring midnight.

Red Blaes
and Blue Moon

AMANDA THOMSON

Edinburgh in the 1980s is a strange, far away, hazy time to think upon and, looking so far back, reflections on where and what and who made us who we are feel partial and vague. Details and events are forgotten or misremembered, timelines confused. Names and faces are blurry. It was Thatcher's Britain still. There were the miners' strike, Red Wedge concerts and Reclaim the Night marches; protests against the poll tax; library sit-ins and demos against the implementation of student loans; rallies supporting the anti-apartheid movement. Boycotts of South Africa were in place and Nelson Mandela was still in prison. The HIV/AIDS epidemic and crisis was incredibly present and for many of us it was a time also defined by Section 28, a law that forbade the promotion of homosexuality, 'pretend family relationships' or anything that was seen to sanction any kind of 'gay lifestyle'. Gayness or queerness in mainstream media, if there at all, was often portrayed as tragic, predatory, or the subject of ridicule.

It seems strange to think back without images readily to hand – in this pre-internet age, there are no images to be found at the flick of a fingertip or through searching an old computer. Any diaries I may have written have been lost or destroyed, most of the photographs too. Time, movement and personal change as we've got older have severed connections, though there are many folk about whom I wonder where life has taken them.

I started studying social sciences at the University of Edinburgh in 1983 and for many of us there was so much to gravitate towards and away from; away from the small towns or smalltown mentalities where we grew up and away from who we were or pretended to be in our youth. Leaving home to go to university was an important movement towards finding out who we might be, and yet becoming ourselves was a complicated business. For many of us from resolutely Scottish working-class places and schools, Edinburgh University was where we suddenly had to negotiate real class differences and privilege for the first time, encountering accents we'd previously only heard reading the BBC News and attitudes and wealth very different from our own. Into this complicated environment we started to discover our gay, Black, queer, feminist selves in ways that hadn't felt possible before, when we'd often been trying to figure things out on our own, and often feeling so much more alone. Still, searching for commonality, understanding difference, accepting and valuing who we were and where we came from was not always straightforward.[1] Moments of gathering, connection and comfort were often transient, and friendship groups intermingled like Venn diagrams as we all tried to figure out the different parts of ourselves, who we were and what we needed.

Somehow, slowly, we gravitated towards others *like us*. Sometimes, at the beginning, it was without even quite knowing why. Each of us, often tentatively, and in our own time, began to find our way to who we were, what-

---

1 A BBC news story saw the headline 'Edinburgh University warns students not to be "snobs"', 11 November 2024, www.bbc.co.uk/news/articles/cx2nyrr16g2o, accessed 27 March 2025

ever that might be, or might become. Maybe some of us left some parts of ourselves behind only to retrieve them later on. We were aware of difference but still trying to figure out what that meant, and our trajectories were often at different speeds too.

For many of us, the gay or gay-friendly places we started to go to were one part of that discovery, places where we just felt somehow comfortable, even if we were not yet out, or if we were yet to act on what and who we thought we might be.

The First of May Bookshop on Candlemaker Row was where we went to get our sociology course books, but inside the shop there was so much to just *come across*. I'm sure I must still have some of the books and pamphlets I bought there, words underlined in pencil and with my scrawled notes in the margins. Audre Lorde's *Zami* and *Sister Outsider*; Adrienne Rich's *Compulsory Heterosexuality and Lesbian Existence*; Barbara Smith's *Toward a Black Feminist Criticism*; *This Bridge Called my Back, Writings by Radical Women of Color*, all opened up new questions and challenges. The First of May sold *Spare Rib* magazines, Women's Press books, the dark green covers of Virago 'modern classics' with the apple on the spine, as well as feminist, gay liberation, CND, anti-apartheid and support-the-miners pamphlets, books and badges – all ways into different ways of thinking and being.

It was a revelation when Scotland's first gay bookshop, Lavender Menace, opened, accessed down a small flight of stairs to a basement shop on Forth Street. Later, when it moved and became West & Wilde on Dundas Street, my recollection is of shelves even more full of the diagonal-striped black and white spines of Women's Press books, an iron between the author and the title; Naiad Press lesbian books from the US too. It's easy, now, to forget what it was like then, how the politics and attitudes of the time made queerness, gayness, lesbianism so much more marginal and invisible; how mainstream bookshops didn't stock the books we could find in the First of May and West & Wilde; how we all had to actively seek out material against a backdrop of legislation that allowed the police to seize books from Gay's the Word in London. Reading itself felt radical, sometimes allowing an informal critique of our university course reading lists, sometimes simply helping us to see ourselves reflected in the world, or future worlds, in ways we had never seen ourselves before. This was a time when lesbians and gays were investigated and hounded out of the military (including someone we knew from 'the scene' who had been based at Edinburgh Castle)[2] and lesbian mothers still feared having their children taken from them.[3]

The poet Joelle Taylor, writing about butch lesbians at that time, has a beautiful part of *C+nto* where she talks about 'three inches of wood between exile and acceptance'.[4] It's the width of the door between the outside world and the entrance to LBGTQ+ pubs and clubs. It's an insight that many of us, whether we regard ourselves as being butch or not, however we define ourselves, understand. These were places where we felt a shift from feeling othered, marginalised or in the minority, to places where we felt both ordinary and extraordinary, where we could love our bodies and how we looked, dress as we wanted to dress, where we felt included and safe to be who we were, in all our diversity.

2 'UK veterans fired over sexuality to get £70,000 in compensation', *The Guardian*, 11 December 2024, www.theguardian.com/world/2024/dec/11/uk-veterans-dismissed-sexuality-lgbt-compensation, accessed 27 March 2025

3 'These women lost their children because they were lesbians – why can't the government say sorry?', *The Guardian*, 18 December 2024, www.theguardian.com/commentisfree/2024/dec/18/lesbian-mothers-scandal-custody-cases-families, accessed 27 March 2025

4 J Taylor, *C+nto: & Othered Poems*, London: The Westbourne Press, 2021

I can still rattle off the names of pubs and places where we came together at that time, places that I've not thought about or been to in years, that were or became part of a lesbian/gay/queer geography of Edinburgh. The biggest and most widely known gay club was Fire Island, a huge venue somewhere along Princes Street, though I don't recall that much about it, and going there just to dance. After the club closed it became a Waterstones bookstore which, as times changed and queerness began its journey to being more mainstream, or mainstream recognised a market, started to stock the very books that we could previously find only in bookshops such as West & Wilde. Other places became spaces to feel safe, to hang with friends and to talk, gossip, fancy folk and laugh. 'Women's nights' tended to be on the quieter weeknights in gay bars when no one else went out, and we considered ourselves lucky to get them: the upstairs bar in Key West on Jamaica Street on a Tuesday night, which was around the corner from the bigger gay bar, The Laughing Duck on Howe Street, which I seem to recall had a club downstairs (sometimes?) on Thursdays. One Friday each month Wilkie House in the Cowgate had a women's disco that later transferred to upstairs at the Playhouse at the top of Leith Walk, and those who came were not just from Edinburgh but gravitated from all over Scotland.

Taylor has another line in *C+nto*, 'she notices that she is sitting at every table', and the feeling of seeing yourself, or your multiple selves, even if there were very few other people of colour, is still something I remember. Seeing ourselves reflected for brief moments in an otherwise heteronormative world, when so many people (more then, perhaps) had to be closeted in everyday life. We drifted in and out of visibility, and to be so visible, so seen, in these moments, meant the world as we could drink, dance, kiss, behave without judgement.

These spaces allowed people to be more themselves, at least for a little while, and I'm sure they saved many lives. The Blue Moon Café, on Broughton Street, where I worked for a while after I graduated and which was opened and run by pals, became a daytime haven and a bustling hub, a place to go to even on our days off. I'm sure at the very beginning the food was made using an old Baby Belling cooker, and everything felt done by the seat of our pants. It was upstairs from the Gay and Lesbian Centre, where a lot of activism and organising took place, and while there were real feelings of anger at that time, there was a sense of optimism and hope for change too. Thinking now of those who were involved in organising the clubs, club nights, marches, protests and buses down to Pride in London, I see just how important their vision and activism was in changing the fabric and easing the path not just for those of us coming out at that time, but in taking forward the battle against hate and for equal rights. I remember still the incredible feeling and pride of being part of Lark in the Park in 1988, out and proud at the Bandstand in Princes Street Gardens, protesting against Section 28, but claiming an everyday visibility too, with Ian McKellen speaking, the magician Fay Presto compering, and feeling empowered enough to mock the God Squad burn-in-hell protesters with their placards damning us all, marching along the pavement above. There's a long trajectory from the 1980s to now, shifts and changes in our communities, visibility, and even legal standing, and we should thank so many of those that came before us, and the places and worlds that they helped create.

Growing up in the 70s and 80s, there were so many ways in which, imperceptibly sometimes, we were expected to behave in certain ways, and there were so many quiet constraints and narrower parameters of how to be a girl or woman. Even if they were loosening all the time, in childhood and adolescence we didn't quite realise it yet, or things hadn't quite reached a small, working-class, Central Belt town. I went to a primary school where girls had to go to a sewing and knitting class when boys got to play football. In secondary school there was a long period of time when girls weren't allowed to wear trousers to school, though I eventually rebelled. I grew up at a time when the Red Top newspapers still had topless page 3 'girls' and Tennent's still had 'lager lovelies' on their beer cans.

For many of us 'different' from the norm in any sort of way, the school gym in the weeks leading up to Christmas was a special kind of hell. Scottish country dancing, where we learned to do the Canadian Barn Dance, the St Bernard's Waltz, the (for many of us, iron-ically named) Gay Gordons, Strip the Willow and the Dashing White Sergeant. The boys lined up on one side of the gym, the girls on the other. The interminable wait for the boys to choose their partners, which they did 99 per cent of the time (apart from when it was 'ladies choice'), accompanied by the feelings of judgement and failure associated with who was picked first or last, then having to find and wear a dress to the Christmas dance. There was so much less queerness, and indeed inclusive multiculturalism, in mainstream life compared to now, even if we might see it sometimes as being co-opted and tokenistic, even though we're still dealing with homo-phobia, misogyny and transphobia.

But sometimes, in order to find one part of yourself, you have to leave other parts behind, at least temporarily, hopefully to rediscover them again if and when needed. So I want to give a shout out to the earlier spaces of my smalltown life where I could be more myself, the places that have remained with me throughout the years and those that I have returned to. Places that weren't queer, but nonetheless gave space for otherness, where we did not have to conform to the more stereotypical tropes of femininity, where we could be ourselves.

I'd like to recognise the playgrounds and the playtimes where I could still go and play football with the boys on the red blaes pitches that defined so many of our Scottish towns, and the gritty skint knees and elbows they gave us. There's often talk of the barriers to experiencing the outdoors and nature for people of colour, for queer people, and for sure, as with everywhere in our lives, we have to deal with occasional homophobia, racism, sexism and heteronormativity. For me, hillwalking and birdwatching gave me places where I could be myself and allowed for the quieter spaces that suit who I am more, and I returned increasingly to such places and activities in adulthood. As a child then teenager, such places and activities freed me from the pressure to wear make-up or the kinds of shoes, skirts, dresses and dress-codes that made me feel so constrained and so alien in my body, where I didn't have to feign an interest in boys. They allowed me a respite from having to actively resist and wonder what I was fighting against, even if I couldn't have articulated that at the time.

And so this essay is also a call to re-claim the non-queer spaces so important for our queer, gay, lesbian and trans bodies, and bodies of colour too. I acknowledge and honour the hillsides, countryside, birds and the natural world that I found my way back to as an adult; the back greens and red blaes football pitches, the dens built and trees climbed and all the places explored on our bikes around my childhood home, and their equivalents throughout Scotland. I'll name the Trossachs and the Arrochar Alps that I explored as part of the hillwalking club at school and the mountains around Crieff where, on a cold winter's day, I experienced my first cloud inversion, emerging from a mist and heading to a peak in bright, cold sunlight while thick cloud blanketed the valleys below; a Field Centre in Perthshire and the Young Ornithologists Club holiday that I went on when I was about 14 with a friend who became, many years later, my first girlfriend, and the dawn stomp we took through the pinewoods looking for capercaillies. By no means queer, places like hillwalking clubs, and for others, sports and athletics clubs, were places where we could dress in ways and act in ways that made us feel like ourselves, even if we weren't out or hadn't even got that far yet. These were the places that I could wear the trousers and walking boots or trainers that did not constrict and made me feel comfortable and capable. Once in Edinburgh, they would morph into the Levi's 501s and Doc Marten boots that made so many of us feel free and strong. These were the places where some of us could just be the tomboys (as we were called then) that were so often the forerunners to our later lesbian, queer or non gender-conforming selves.

Sm:)e for 2004

MJ DEANS

Welcome to Cumbernauld. It's 2003. You're 14 and about to make the journey from Condorrat to Kildrum for your first night as a member of the Senior Youth Theatre. Technically, you're three months too young to move into this class, but you've planned a whole story if anyone questions it, which they won't (you hope).

You ask your mum when you'll be driving over, and she tells you that you can get a bus, you're old enough now. There's £2 at the door which will be enough for a single and your dad will collect you at the end of the night. This is good, no one will question you being three months too young if you arrive on your own.

You check yourself in the mirror before you leave. Brown hair, straightened – you snuck into your sister's room earlier to use her GHDs. Mouth full of braces. A pair of baby blue cargo trousers and a pastel pink Paul Frank tank top (the top was part of a pyjama set you got for your birthday, but it's too cute not to wear out the house). Satisfied, you run out the door.

On the bus, you bump into a couple of folk you know from the Wednesday night youth cafe at the Link Centre. They're smoking, so you sit in front of them, hoping to soak up a bit of the smell. Smoking is so fifteen-year-old. They ask where you're off to in between puffs, and you smile as you tell them you're off to the Youth Theatre.

'Sounds gay.' They laugh. It's 2003 and everything

different is gay. 'I'm not gay, but it's cool if you are,' they say, and you all laugh together.

You get off the bus and make your way down through the housing areas and flats. You've only ever gotten a lift to the theatre before and the walking route isn't very well sign-posted, especially in the near-dark. You decide to ask for directions in the wee shop, and you can pick up a packet of Space Raiders and a tin of Tizer with your leftover bus fare while you are there.

You follow the directions the man in the shop gave you down the hill away from the bus stop, along the blocks of flats with their brick balconies, pass the grassy common area, and into the back of the car park.

And there it is. At the bottom of the hill, surrounded by trees. A white, squashed bungalow. Looking more like a row of farm cottages than a theatre (which, to be fair, is exactly what it started life as back in the 1800s,[1] years before you were born). The shutters are open and a warm glow spills out onto the path from the windows of the top bar on the left and the studio theatre on the right. The top bar has its own entrance a few metres down from the main one, but you can see a few regulars inside enjoying their pints and fags. The bottom bar further inside the building through the main doors won't be open tonight as there's not a show on, so maybe you'll get to use its labyrinthine space to rehearse some scenes.

It got fully dark in between your visit to the shop and here, and leaves crunch under your feet as you make your way down to the double doors. A few teenagers of various sizes, genders and fashion senses are also arriving; getting dropped off by parents or following behind you down the

1 M Glendinning and D M Watters, 'Cumbernauld' in R Close, J Gifford and F Arneil Walker, *The Buildings of Scotland: Lanarkshire and Renfrewshire*, New Haven and London: Yale University Press, 2016, p243

path from the bus stop. They are rowdy with each other, but not unfriendly. You have a feeling in your belly like nerves, but the good kind. Most of the teenagers are a fair bit older than you (by three months at least) and you've seen some of them in plays. But you know more than a few of them from school, the youth cafe and the younger youth theatre classes, so you're not too over-whelmed. They seem exactly like your flavour of people, and you smile your brace-filled smile. The good-nervy feeling in your belly gets stronger as you are welcomed by the people you know, and introduced to the ones you don't. Some of them are *hot*. Bonus.

One boy shakes your hand. He's wearing a Wolverine t-shirt. Another boy, tall and slim with fair hair, holds the doors open for you. The sound of laughter and chairs scraping along a wooden floor hits your eardrums. You don't know it yet, but the course of your life has just been irrevocably altered.

You step inside.

*

After the final Christmas show of the 2019 season, Cumbernauld Theatre closed to the public for good, never again to open on its site among the trees at the bottom of Braehead Road. We all know what happened in 2020, and for that and various other reasons, the old building fell into decay over the next few years. Sometime in 2023, the entire back half was demolished, leaving only the original farm cottages.

If you had entered these farm cottages through the main doors when the theatre was still open, you could have turned right and gone into the Brian Miller Studio; a small black box space that would seat well under 100 people, that was mostly used in the later years by community groups and as rehearsal space. Or instead, you could have gone left past the box office to find yourself in the top bar, a cosy wee place that always had a good tune on and a friendly member of staff ready to give you a cheap pint. These spaces are all that remain of the old Cumbernauld Theatre. The 250 seat auditorium which was added on in the 1970s (one of the few Scottish theatres in a 'thrust' configuration, meaning the audience sat around the stage on three sides), its backstage areas and the bottom bar are now all gone. The Cumbernauld Theatre signage still remains near the main doors however, letting anyone who might happen to pass by know that these strange decrepit cottages once had another life. The word Cumbernauld is now smeared, and someone has graffitied FCK NZS on the image. I like to think this would have tickled the group of artists and volunteers who started the theatre, then known as the Cottage Theatre,[2] in the 1960s.

While Cumbernauld is one of Scotland's five New Towns, it didn't just appear by magic in the 1960s. Cumbernauld (coming from the Gaelic Comar nan Allt, meaning the meeting of the waters) as a settlement can be traced back to Roman times. You can visit the remains of the Antonine Wall in Croy, and a few miles down the road in Kildrum you can find Cumbernauld House, built on the site of the former Cumbernauld Castle, visited by Mary Queen of Scots. The theatre cottages were originally built as part of this estate, and I often wonder what the people who lived back then would make of the town now. Would they care that it had been awarded the Plook on the Plinth award for 'most dismal town in Scotland' (twice,

---

2   Historic Environment Scotland Listed Buildings Portal, 'Cumbernauld Theatre' (17 January 2024), portal.historicenvironment.scot/, accessed 14 November 2024

and nominated a third time)? What would they make of Irn Bru, lovingly bottled in Cumbernauld? How would they react to folk saying 'What's it called?' every time they tell someone where they're from thanks to an advert from the 1980s? To be fair, I think they'd be as perplexed as I am to this day at the thought of a town advertising itself on the television with its own catchphrase. Probably they'd be too busy, likely with mining or weaving which were the local industries of the time, to put much thought into the identity of the place. But when the Cottage Theatre opened in February 1963 in the shiny modern Cumbernauld, I imagine that was exactly the question the founding artists and volunteers were asking themselves. Not 'What's it called?', but rather what could Cumbernauld be?

There's not a lot of information about those early days, or exactly how the volunteers transformed the old cottages into a venue for the community. These were people such as Brian Miller, Cumbernauld's appointed Town Artist, and Tom Laurie, who continued to have an impact on culture in Scotland at the Scottish Arts Council, the Traverse Theatre and the Tron Theatre. These founders were pretty radical and anti-establishment. According to stand-up comedian Stu Who?, he was just a 'mohawk-sporting nutter who fronted a very anarchistic, local band' when he was offered the leading role in one of Brian Miller's plays at the theatre, without any prior acting experience.[3] The volunteers went into an historic building, made a theatre and created art, for, with and by their new found community.

Community spirit was always strong in the theatre in my experience. When I joined CYT in 1999 (Cumbernauld Youth Theatre that is, not to be confused with the Carbrain

3   Stu Who? WordPress Blog, 'Cumbernauld Theatre' (9 November 2015), stuwho.wordpress.com/tag/cumbernauld-theatre, accessed 14 November 2024

Young Team), it was only thanks to Terri Jones who ran the Youth Theatre secretly agreeing to allow my parents to pay £3 per class each week, instead of the upfront £30 a term you were supposed to. At that point in my family history, paying a £30 fee upfront would have been impossible. Without that seemingly small kindness to allow me into the world of theatre, I might have started down an altogether different and much less happy path in life (potentially a better paying one to be fair).

When I went back to teach at the youth theatre as an adult, I was delighted to discover they'd hardly put the prices up. I was offering the exact same workshops for Cumbernauld Theatre as I was for Scottish Youth Theatre at the time, but at SYT you would pay more than three times the price. Theatre and the arts can have a profound transformative power on young people, which I understand because of the effect they had on me and my fellow youth theatre members.

Cumbernauld Theatre always took me in, whether I was too poor or (three months) too young.

*

The boy in the Wolverine t-shirt asks if you'd like a tour of the theatre. You've been coming here for years, so of course you don't *need* one, but you love the X-Men so you say yes. You suspect he might even know you don't need a tour, and you swallow involuntarily.

You follow behind him into the studio. You feel your nose close up almost instantly, it always does in this ancient space. The exposed bricks on the outer wall that every adventurous kid loved to try and climb, you included, are always throwing dust into the air, as are the old wooden beams above you.

Ten years from now, you'll teach drama classes for children in this space. It will feel like coming home, and you'll love it. Somehow, the children will know you better than you know yourself and they'll teach you so many important things (least of which, maybe that furry leopard print jacket wasn't a good idea after all, thanks kids). You and the children will share many moments of great joy and freedom together. When you're no longer able to commit to teaching there because of tour schedules and life, you'll miss it so very much. You'll treasure those young people and the friends you worked with, and that old, dusty space and all the memories it holds.

The boy in the Wolverine t-shirt leads you down stage right and you both stand about a metre from the door to the backstage areas. *This is where we'll have our first kiss, in two months time*, he tells you. *The director will be watching from nearby and you'll be so nervous you'll think you're vibrating. Our lips will barely touch and it'll be perfect.*

You walk with him through the door and down to the backstage areas. You turn right and follow the bunker-like corridor into the upstage left wing, where your eyes take a moment to adjust to the darkness. A couple of years from now, you'll run in here to calm down after forgetting your lines during a show. You're fairly sure the audience didn't notice, but it will be one of the most terrifying experiences of your short life. Thanks to your experiences on that stage, you'll pretty much be the first person off-book in any show after that, knowing your lines inside out, and quick to jump in and help if someone else dries.

You both continue your journey backstage, travelling together stage right, past the haunted staircase where the spirit of the Snow Queen resides (a jealous actress pushed her down the stairs apparently, stories vary from person to person) and into the boys' dressing room. This room has an amber hue and a close kind of quiet. You feel like you shouldn't be in here, but it's just a quick stop for him to point out the famous sight. Stuck to the roof is the expertly removed gooey centre of a Jaffa Cake. Whoever got it up there must have taken their time, slowly nibbling round the chocolate and sponge while protecting the structural integrity of the jammy disc. *It's been up there for a hundred years*, he whispers. *And it'll be up there for a hundred more*. Whoever got it up there has become a legend.

Onwards to the girls' dressing room. This space has the same orange glow, but in here the colour and silence bring peace. This room has seen so much laughter, and tears, and nerves, and jealousy, and anxiety. It offers the comfort of a tired old mattress that fits your body perfectly. This time it's the boy's turn to feel uncomfortable, but he seems better at hiding it than you. That, or he genuinely is at ease here, the slut.

Together, you leave and enter the vomitorium, or the Vom as everyone calls it. Growing up in a theatre with a Vom, it seemed so normal, but in all the shows and all the tours you'll go on to do as an adult, you'll never encounter another theatre with one. Every theatre should have a Vom. The best thing about it is that you can stand right in the middle and look out onto the stage without being seen, getting the perfect end-on view of the action. As long as you're quiet of course – the audience sit right above your head (this is also why you have to pick the perfect moment to go for a mid-show pee, the pipes run right under their feet). The Vom is where you'll take all your pictures in costume, where Julie will film those precious behind-the-scenes home movies, a perfect time capsule of the moment, where you'll dance hidden from the audience but in full view of the kids in your class in case they forget their dance moves. The magic of what makes this specific theatre in this specific town in this specific country in this specific time is strongest here.

You look up, and you can see someone has written something right above the tunnel-like entrance to the stage. It says 'Oh ... The Glamour of it all'.

*

Like most children (and teenagers, and humans in general), I could be very preoccupied with my identity. I spent a lot of time feeling like I was stuck between different worlds and identities, never quite able to fully commit to one label or community or another. I felt too Gaelic for the English-speaking kids – like I had the wrong accent for the Gaels – I'd kissed too many girls to be straight – definitely kissed too many boys to be gay – not feminine enough to carry off that look – too girlie to be into that game. I remember crying into my *Bunty* magazine while wearing my *Matrix* t-shirt one afternoon because I felt so wrong. I should be into *Bunty* or *The Matrix*, not both. All I wanted was to be able to fit neatly into a labelled box and feel good about it, but please don't make me make a decision or I'll cry.

Looking back now, I know it seems silly. But young MJ just wanted to belong. At CYT I did, I belonged to that theatre in the trees and the group of misfits that ran in like tornados every Tuesday and Thursday evening. I didn't worry about school there, or home, or who I might be each day. Any quirk of my personality was lost in a sea of even weirder teenagers who I loved dearly, and anyway, why would personal shortcomings matter when you could instead be a witch, or a swordsman, or an orphan, or a ringmaster? Try something else tomorrow if it doesn't fit, there are no wrong answers and you're brave for trying.

As an adult, I'm less worried about fitting in boxes. I know myself well enough now to realise that I am fickle and change my mind and mood easily. I used to prefer the label bi, but now I'm more comfortable with queer. I used to refer to myself as an actress, and then I hated that and how dare you call me an actress when I'm an actor, and wait, I quite like actress again. So now, I just try to find communities to be part of that enrich my soul. Who cares what you call me, it'll be different tomorrow anyway.

My whole life I've only ever been able to commit fully to two things: my passion for theatre, and the boy in the Wolverine t-shirt. Both of which were given to me by the community at Cumbernauld Theatre.

*

The tour has come to an end. You and the boy with the Wolverine t-shirt step out onto the stage to find it busy, full of the hormones and terrible chat of Cumbernauld's finest young people. The director is trying to gather everyone in a circle for a warm-up game, so you can learn each other's names. This will be important; some of these names you'll want to remember for the rest of your life.

You listen carefully to the instructions for the game, not wanting to make a mistake and possibly draw attention to the fact you're (three months) too young to be here. Turns out you've played this game before, and with your excellent reflexes from years of Nintendo, you're not worried about being shot with finger guns tonight.

As you listen for your name, or the names of the people on either side of you (Rachel, Caitlin), you study the group through the haze of the theatre lights and consider this space that you all share together.

Your time here with these people will be unfairly brief. Soon the This-Here-Now will become the That-There-Then. In a year, you'll travel to Manchester together to perform at the Contacting the World festival, where you'll meet youth theatres from Syria, Bangladesh, Pakistan, Nigeria. This experience will inform your whole view of the world and the arts, and you'll kiss someone from Jordan and keep forgetting their name as they tell you they're going to get your name tattooed on their arm before the plane home. In three years you will have left the youth theatre to study Acting at college and the boy with the fair hair who held the doors open for you will be gone. A year after that you will all return here with sunflowers to remember him.

And then, a lifetime of more. You'll change. You'll grow. You'll love. You'll be a bit of a dick. You'll fuck up. You'll try on various labels for yourself, and collect or discard them as you see fit. Most importantly, you will allow yourself to be terrible at the things you want to try without fear. You'll experience such joy and wonder and rage and privilege, and you will navigate yourself through it all thanks to the experiences and the people you met at Cumbernauld Youth Theatre.

In twenty-one years you'll be writing this, smiling. infinitely grateful for the local theatre among the trees that took you in.

*

Cumbernauld Theatre has a new building now. It sits about a mile down the road from its old site, attached to Cumbernauld High School. The new building opened in

October 2021 and offers the residents of the New Town not only two separate spaces to watch theatre, but also a dance studio and a cinema. For as long as I've been alive, Cumbernauld and its roughly 50,000 residents has not had a cinema.

While new buildings can often lack personality and spirit, I think the soul and ethos of the old building is still there, for those willing to look. I hope there is a girl in there right now, learning about herself and falling in love and figuring out what labels fit her and I hope the new Cumbernauld Theatre will be there for her as she makes her way in the world.

In October 2024, the boy in the Wolverine t-shirt and I went back to visit what remained of the old building. The space where the auditorium, the Vom, the sacred Jaffa Cake and the haunted staircase once were is now an empty grassy waste ground. Wildflowers grow out of the earth. The remaining farm cottages lie among the trees between the car park and the dual carriageway. Those farm cottages have stood for 250 years, and when they finally succumb to time and decay, I hope wildflowers will grow there too.

Sm:)e airson 2004

MJ DEANS

Fàilte gu Comar nan Allt. 'S e 2003 a th' ann. Tha thu ceithir bliadhna deug a dh'aois agus tha thu gus a bhith deiseil airson an turais a dhèanamh bho Chon-dobhrait gu Cill Druim airson a' chiad oidhche agad mar bhall de Theatar na h-Òigridh. Gu h-onarach, tha thu trì mìosan ro òg airson a bhith anns a' chlas seo, ach tha thu air deagh sgeulachd a chur ri chèile ma chuireas duine ceist ort mu dheidhinn, ach cha chuir (tha thu an dòchas).

Tha thu a' faighneachd dha do mhàthair cuin a bhios sibh a falbh anns a' chàr, agus tha i ag innse dhut gun urrainn dhut am bus fhaighinn, tha thu sean gu leòr a-nis. Tha £2 aig an doras 's bhiodh sin pailteas airson aon rathad agus togaidh d' athair thu aig deireadh na h-oidhche. Deagh bheachd, cha bhi ceist aig duine gu bheil thu trì miosan ro òg ma bhios tu a' nochdadh ann leat fhèin.

Tha thu a' toirt sùil ort fhèin anns an sgàthan mus fhalbh thu. Falt donn, dìreach – ghoid thu a-steach dha rùm do pheathar airson mèirle a dhèanamh air na straight-eners aice. Beul làn de thaic-fhiaclan. Briogais cargo soilleir-ghorm agus lèine tanc taois-phinc Paul Frank (bha an lèine mar pairt de sheata deise-leapa, ach tha i ro cute airson a bhith ga cumail anns an taigh). Riaraichte, leumaidh tu a-mach air an doras.

Air a' bhus, coinnichidh tu ri dithis air a bheil thu eòlach bhon youth cafe a tha a' gabhail àite air oidhche Diciadain aig an Link Centre. Tha iad a' smocadh, 's leis an sin suidhidh tu air am beulaibh, làn dòchais gum biodh am fàileadh a' fuireach air d' aodach. Smoking is so fifteen-years-old. Tha iad a' faighneachd càite bheil thu a' dol fhad 's a tha iad a' smùdadh, agus tha thu a' dèanamh gàire nuair a chanas tu gu bheil thu a' dol dhan Youth Theatre. 'Coltas gèidh air sin.' Tha iad a' gàireachdainn. 'S e 2003 a th' ann, agus tha a h-uile rud a tha eadar-dhealaichte gèidh. 'Chan eil mi gèidh, ach tha cool ma tha thusa,' tha iad ag ràdh agus tha sibh uile a' gàireachdainn còmhla.

Tha thu a' faighinn dhen bhus agus a' tòiseachadh air do shlighe sìos tron ionad-thaighean. Cha tàinig thu air a' bhus dhan theatre a-riamh, agus chan eil an slighe-stiùiridh uabhasach soilleir, gu h-àraidh anns a' chamhanaich. Ròghnaich thu gun tèid thu a-steach dhan bhùth bhig gus stiùireadh fhaighinn, 's urrainn dhut pacaid Space Raiders agus can de Tizer fhaighinn cuideachd le na tha air fhàgail bhon airgead airson a' bhus fhad 's a tha thu ann.

Tha thu a' leantainn an stiùiridh a fhuair thu bhon fhear anns a' bhùth shìos an cnoc, bus ri bus ri na flataichean leis na for-àraidhean breige aca, seachad air a' ghlas choiteanta, agus a-staigh air cùl na pàirc-chàraichean.

Agus sin e. Aig bonn a' chnuic am measg chraobhan. Bungalo geal, pliachd. Nas fhaisge gu riadh taighean-tu-athanais an Taigh-Cluiche (agus gu bhith cothromach, 's e sin a bh' annta aig an toiseach anns na 1800,[1] bliadhna-ichean mus do rugadh tu). Tha na for-uinneagan fosgailte, agus tha luisnich bhlàth a' dòrtadh a-mach air an ràs bhon bhàr uachdar air an taobh chlì agus an stiùideo air an taobh dheas. Tha doras eadar-dhealaichte aig a' bhàr uach-dair, dha no trì meatairean bhon priomh fhear, ach faodaidh tu feadhainn a-staigh fhaicinn ag òl pinnt agus

---

1   M Glendinning agus D M Watters, 'Cumbernauld' ann an R Close, J Gifford agus F Arneil Walker, *The Buildings of Scotland: Lanarkshire and Renfrewshire*, New Haven and London: Yale University Press, 2016, td243

a' smocadh. Cha bhi am bàr ìochdar fosgailte a-nochd air
sgàth 's nach eil 'show' air, 's leis an sin 's dòcha gum b'
urrainn dhut an spàs cuartain a chleachdadh airson seallaidhean a chur ri chèile.

Dh'fhas e dubh dorcha eadar an àm a thàinig thu a-mach
às a' bhùth agus a-nis, agus tha duillich a' cnagadh fo do
chasan fhad 's a tha thu a' coiseachd sìos dhan doras. Tha
buidheann de dheugairean le meudan, gnèithean agus
fasanan eadar-dhealaichte a' nochdadh cuideachd; a-mach
à càraichean phàrantan agus a' tighinn air do chùlaibh
bhon stad-bus. Tha iad ròlaiseach le chèile, ach chan eil
iad neo-chàirdeil. Tha faireachdainn agad nad bhrù coltach
ri nuair a tha thu nearbhasach, ach 's e faireachdainn math
a th' ann. Tha a' mhòr-chuid de na deugairean fada nas
sine na thusa (trì miosan nas sine co-dhiù), agus tha thu
air feadhainn fhaicinn ann an dealbhan-cluiche. Ach tha
thu eòlach air barrachd na dithis bhon sgoil, an cafaidh
òigridh air oidhche Chiadain agus na clasaichean nas òige
anns an talla-cluiche, 's leis an sin chan eil thu ro
iomagaineach. Tha coltas orra mar gur iad an seòrsa dhaoine
air a bheil thu glè mheasail, agus tha thu a' dèanamh gàire
le do beul làn taic-fhiaclan. Tha am faireachdainn nad bhrù
a' fàs nas treasa fhad 's a tha an fheadhainn air a bheil thu
eòlach a' cur fàilte ort, agus tha thu a' coinneachadh ris
an fheadhainn eile airson a' chiad triop. Tha aon no dha
dhiubh *hot*. 'S e duais a tha sin.

Tha aon bhalach a' crathadh do làimh. Tha lèine
Wolverine air. Tha balach eile, àrd agus caol le falt bàn a'
fosgladh an dorais air do shon. Tha am fuaim de gàireachdainn agus seithrichean gan slaodadh thairis air làr fiodha
a' bualadh ort. Chan eil fhios agad air seo fhathast, ach
tha an cùrsa-beatha agad dìreach air atharrachadh gun
tilleadh.

Tha thu a' gabhail ceum a-steach.

*

As dèidh cuirm-chluiche na Nollaig dheireannaich ann an 2019, dhùin na dorsan aig Taigh-cluiche Chomar nan Allt airson an turais mu dheireadh, agus cha do dh'fhosgail iad dhan mhòr-shluagh bhon làraich am measg nan craobhan aig bonn Rathad Braehead gu bràth tuilleadh. Tha sinn uile làn eolach air na thachair ann an 2020, agus air sgàth sin agus adhbharan eile, thòisich an seann togalach a' crìonadh thairis air na bliadhaichean ri teachd. Uaireigin ann an 2023, chaidh an leth aig cùl an togalaich a leagail, a' fàgail nan taighean-tuathanais far an robh am bàr uachdar agas an stiùideo a-mhàin.

Nuair a bha an taigh-cluiche fhathast fosgailte, nam biodh tu air a dhol a-steach do na taighean-tuathanais tro na prìomh dhorsan, dh'fhaodadh tu tionndadh chun na làimhe deise agus a dhol a-steach do Stiùidio Brian Miller; àite beag dubh airson nas lugha na 100 duine, a bha air a chleachdadh anns na bliadhnaichean mu dheireadh le buidhnean coimhearsnachd agus mar àite ro-aithris. No, dh'fhaodadh tu a dhol clì seachad air oifis nan tiogaidean gus thu fhèin a lorg anns a' bhàr uachdar, àite beag cofhurtail air an robh deagh fhonn agus neach-obrach càirdeil deiseil airson pinnt a thoirt dhut. Is iad na h-àiteannan a tha air fhàgail de sheann Taigh-cluiche Chomar nan Allt. An t-ionad-èisteachd airson 250 duine a chaidh a thogail anns na seachdadan (aon de na h-aon taighean-cluiche 'thrust' ann an Alba, a' ciallachadh gun robh an luchd-eisteachd a' suidhe mun cuairt air trí taobhan), raon obrach cùl an àrd-ùrlar agus am bàr ìochdar, tha iad uile dì-làraichte a-nis. Tha an sanas Taigh-Cluiche Chomar nan Allt fhathast ann faisg air na dorsan, a' toirt fiosrachadh do dhuine sam bith a' dol seachad gun robh beatha eadar-dhealaichte aig an togalach àraid seo aig aon àm.

Tha am facal Comar nan Allt air a liacadh a-nis, agus tha cuideigin air graffitti FCK NZS a sgrìobhadh air an ìomhaigh. Bu toil leam bhith smaoineachadh gum biodh na saor-thoilich a thòisich an Taigh-Cluiche anns na seasgadan, ainmichte 'The Cottage Theatre'[2] aig an àm sin, toilichte leis an seo.

Ged a tha Comar nan Allt mar aon de na 5 Bailtean Ùra ann an Alba, cha do nochd e le draoidheachd anns na 60an. Chithear Comar nan Allt mar àite-tuineachaidh air ais gu àm nan Ròmanach. Faodaidh tu tadhal air na tha air fhàgail de Bhalla Antonine ann an Crothaidh, agus beagan mhìltean sìos an rathad ann an Cill Druim lorgaidh tu Taigh Chomar nan Allt, a chaidh a thogail air làrach seann Chaisteal Chomar nan Allt air an do thadhail Màiri Banrigh na h-Alba. Chaidh na taighean-tuathanais far an deach an Taigh-Cluiche a thogail an toiseach mar phàirt den stàid seo, agus bidh e tric a' cur iongnadh orm dè a bhiodh na daoine a bha a' fuireach aig an àm sin a' smaoineachadh mu dheidhinn a' bhaile a-nis. Am biodh dragh orra gun deach duais Plook on the Plinth a dhuaiseachadh air airson 'most dismal town in Scotland' (dà uair, agus ainmeachadh an treas uair)? Dè am beachd a bhiodh aca air Irn Bru, air a' bhotalachadh le gaol ann an Comar nan Allt? Ciamar a dhèiligeadh iad ri daoine ag ràdh 'What's it called?' a h-uile turas a dh'innseas iad do chuideigin cò às a tha iad, air sgàth 's sanas bho na 80an? Leis an fhìrinn innse, tha mi a' smaoineachadh gum biodh e na chùis-iongnaidh dhaibhsan mar a tha e dhomh fhèin chun an latha an-diugh gun robh baile ga shanasachd fhèin air an telebhisean leis an abairt aige fhèin. Is dòcha gum biodh iad ro thrang le mèinneadh no figheadaireachd a bha nan gnìomhachasan ionadail aig an àm, airson mòran smao-

---

2   Historic Environment Scotland Listed Buildings Portal, 'Cumbernauld Theatre' (17 Faoilleach 2024), portal.historicenvironment.scot/, ruigsinneach 14 Samhain 2024

ineachaidh a dhèanamh air dearbh-aithne an àite. Ach nuair a dh' fhosgail an Cottage Theatre sa Ghearran 1963 ann an Comar nan Allt ùr-fhasanta gleansach, tha mi a' smaoineachadh gur e sin an dearbh cheist a bha an luchd-stèidheachaidh agus na saor-thoilich a' faighneachd dhaibh fhèin. Chan e 'What's it called?' ach dè a dh'fhaodadh Comar nan Allt a bhith?

Chan eil tòrr fiosrachaidh ann mu dheidhinn nan laithean tràtha sin, no ciamar a rinn na saor-thoilich cruth-atharrachadh air na taighean-tuathanais gus Taigh-Cluiche a thogail dhan choimhearsnachd. Daoine mar Brian Miller, Neach-Ealain Oifigeil do Chomar nan Allt, agus Tom Laurie, a lean a' toirt buaidh air cultur ann an Alba aig Coimhairle nan Ealain, an Traverse agus an Tron. Bha na stèidheadairean seo gu tur radaigeach agus anti-establishment. A rèir fear-comaig Stu Who?, cha robh e ach 'mohawk-sporting nutter who fronted a very anarchistic, local band' nuair a thug Brian Miller am priomh phairt anns an dealbh-chluich ùr aige dha, gun eòlas sam bith aige air a bhith air an àrd-ùrlar.[3]

Chaidh na saor-thoilich seo a-steach do thogalach eachdrachail, rinn iad Taigh-Cluiche agus chruthaich iad ealain airson agus leis a' choimhearsnachd ùr aca.

Bha an spiorad coimhearsnachd seo a-riamh làidir aig an Taigh-Cluiche bho m' fhèin-fhiosrachadh. Nuair a thòisich mi aig CYT (Cumbernauld Youth Theatre, chan e Carbrain Young Team) ann an 1999, bha còir agad £30 a phàigheadh gach teirm. Aig an àm sin, bha mo theaghlach neo-chomasach air sin a dheanamh, agus 's e an t-aon adhbhar gun robh cead agam pàirt a ghabhail, gun do rinn Terri Jones a bha os cionn an Tèatar Òigridh cùmhnant dìomhair le mo mhàthair. Phàigh sinn £3 gach

---

3 Stu Who? Bloga WordPress, 'Cumbernauld Theatre' (9 Samhain 2015), stuwho.wordpress.com/tag/cumbernauld-theatre, ruigsinneach 14 Samhain 2024

clas an àite £30 gach teirm, agus mura robh mi air an gnìomh beag còir sin fhaighinn gus cothram fhaighinn air ceum a thoirt a-steach dhan t-saoghal tèatar, 's dòcha gum bithinn air rathad beatha eadar-dhealaichte mì-thoil-ichte a-nis (ach 's dòcha cuideachd gum bithinn air rathad beatha le pàigheadh nas fhèarr).

Nuair a chaidh mi air ais dhan Taigh-Cluiche mar inbheach airson teagaisg san tèatar òigridh, bha mi air mo dhoigh nuair a lorg mi a-mach cha mhòr nach robh iad air a' chosgais a chur suas idir. Bha mi a' teagaisg na h-aon bhùithtean obrach aig Scottish Youth Theatre 's a bha mi aig CYT, ach dh'fheumadh tu pàigheadh air a shon aig SYT. Tha cumhachd cruth-atharrachail domhain aig tèatar agus na h-ealain air daoine òga, rud a tha mi a' tuigsinn leis a' bhuaidh a thug iad ormsa agus air mo cho-bhuill theatar òigridh, agus cha bu chòir cosgais a bhith na chnap-starra air ruigsinneachd do dhuine sam bith.

Thug Taigh-Cluiche Chomar nan Allt a-steach mi an-còmhnaidh, a dh'aindeoin gun robh mi ro bhochd no (trì miosan) ro òg.

*

Tha am balach ann an lèine Wolverine a' faighneachd a bheil thu ag iarraidh cuairt den Taigh-Cluiche. Tha thu air a bhith tighinn dhan àite seo airson bliadhnaichean, 's mar sin gun teagamh chan eil thu feumach air fear, ach 's fìor thoigh leat na X-Men 's leis an sin tha thu a cantainn seadh. Tha amharas agad gu bheil fios aige nach eil thu feumach air cuairt cuideachd, agus tha thu dèanamh slug gun a bhith feuchainn.

Leanaidh tu air a chùlaibh a-steach don stiùidio. Tha do shròn a' dùnadh cha mhòr a' mhionaid a chuir thu ceum a-steach an seo, mar as àbhaist anns an rùm seanndaidh seo. Tha na breigichean fosgailte air a' bhalla air an robh a h-uile leanabh dàna a' còrdadh ri bhith sreap, thu fhèin cuideachd, agus na seann sailean fiodha os a chionn an-còmhnaidh a' tilgeil dust dhan adhar.

Deich bhliadhna bho seo, bidh thu a' teagasg chlasaichean dràma do dh'òigridh anns an àite seo. Bidh thu a' faireachdainn mar gu bheil thu a' tilleadh dhachaigh agus còrdaidh e riut gu mòr. Dòigh air choreigin, bidh a' chlann eòlach ort nas fheàrr na tha thu eòlach ort fhèin agus ionnsaichidh iad dhut iomadh rud cudromach (gu h-àraidh, is dòcha às deidh a h-uile càil nach b' e deagh bheachd a bh' anns an t-seacaid bian leopard print sin, taing kids). Bidh thu fhèin agus a' chlann co-roinneadh tòrr mhòmaidean de dh'aoibhneas agus saorsa còmhla. Nuair nach urrainn dhut a bhith a' teagasg an sin tuilleadh air sgàth clàran-siubhail agus beatha, bidh tu ga ionndrainn gu mòr. Bidh na daoine òga sin, agus na caraidean leis an robh thu ag obair, ionmhainn leat, mar a bhios an t-àite sean, dustach sin agus na cuimhneachain a tha na bhroinn.

Tha am balach ann an lèine Wolverine gad stiùreadh deas downstage agus tha an dithis agaibh a' seasamh mu meadrachd bhon doras dhan raon obrach cùl an àrd-ùrlar. *Seo far am bi a' chiad phòg againn, ann mu dhà mhìos,* tha e ag innse dhut. *Bidh an stiùiriche a' coimhead bho faisg air làimh, agus bidh tu cho nearbhach bidh thu a' faireachdainn mar gu bheil thu air chrith. Cha mhòr gum bean ar bilean ri chèile agus bidh e foirfichte.*

Tha thu a' coiseachd còmhla ris tron doras agus sìos dhan raon obrach cùl an àrd-ùrlar. Tha thu a' dol deas agus a' leantainn an trannsa coltach ri buncair dhan cùl clì upstage. Bliadhna no dhà bho seo, ruithidh tu an seo gus socair a ghabhail às dèidh nam faclan agad a dhìochuimhneachadh air an àrd-ùrlar. Nì thu do dhicheall agus cha mhothaich an luchd-èisteachd idir, ach is e an rud as eagalaiche a thachair dhut nad bheatha ghoirid a bhios ann. Taing don eòlas a fhuair thu air an àrd-ùrlar sin, 's tusa a' chiad duine 'off-book' ann an dealbh-cluich sam bith anns a bheil thu às dèidh sin, cho eòlach air na faclan agad 's tha thu air ùrlar do thaighe, agus a' chiad duine airson cuideachadh a thoirt do chuideigin eile ma tha iad steigte.

Tha an dithis agaibh a' cumail oirbh air an taisteal agaibh air cùl an àrd-ùrlair, a' siubhal deas, seachad air far a bheil spiorad an Snow Queen air tathaich na staidhre (phut bana-chleasaiche eudach sìos an staidhre i a rèir choltais, tha sgeulachd eadar-dhealaichte aig gach duine), agus a-steach dha seòmar-èididh nam balach. Tha seòrsa de sholas buidhe-shoilleir anns an rùm seo, agus sàmhchas a tha faisg ann an dòigh. Tha thu a' faireachdainn mar nach bu chòir dhut a bhith ann an seo, ach cha bhi sibh ann ach airson ùine ghoirid, tha e dìreach airson an sealladh ainmeil a shealltainn dhut. Steigte ris a' mhullach, tha thu a' faicinn meadhan steigeach grinn Jaffa Cake.

Ge bith cò a thilg e suas an sin, feumaidh gun tug iad an ùine slaodach ag ithe timcheall an teoclaid is an spong fhad 's a bha iad a' cumail a' mheadhain jammy ann an aon chnap. *Tha e air a bhith shuas an sin airson ceud bliadhna*, chagair e. *Agus bidh e shuas airson ceud a bharrachd.* Ge bith cò a rinn sin, feumaidh gur e uirsgeul a bh' annta.

Coisichidh sibh romhaibh, dha seòmar-èididh nan nigheanan. Tha an aon solas buidhe-shoilleir ri lorg an seo, ach an seo tha an dath agus an sàmhchair a' toirt fois dhut. Tha an rùm seo air cus gàireachdainn, deòir, iomlasg, agus eudachd fhaicinn. Tha e a' tabhann dhut an aon seòrsa cofhurtachd 's a gheibh thu bho sheann mhatras a tha a' freagairt air do bhodhaig gu foirfe. An turas seo, bu chòir dhan bhalach faireachdainn mar nach eil cead aige a bhith an seo, ach tha esan nas fhèarr air sin a chur air falach. No 's dòcha gu bheil e dha-rìribh cofhurtail a-staigh an seo, an t-siùrsach.

Le chèile, tha sibh a' falbh agus a' gabhail a-steach dhan vomitorium, no The Vom mar a chanas a h-uile duine. Nuair a tha thu air a thogail ann an Taigh-Cluiche le vomitorium tha e cho cumanta, ach anns a h-uile tais-beanadh agus a h-uile turas air an tèid thu mar inbheach, chan fhaic thu Taigh-Cluiche eile le fear. Bu chòir dha Vom a bhith anns gach Taigh-Cluiche. 'S e an rud as fhèarr mu dheidhinn, gum b' urrainn dhut seasamh anns an teis-meadhan agus coimhead air na tha a' tachairt air an àrd-ùrlar gun a bhith air d' fhaicinn. Cho fada 's a tha thu sàmhach gun teagamh — tha an luchd-èisteachd nan suidhe dìreach os cionn do chinn (seo cuideachd carson a dh'fheumas tu a' mhòmaid cheart a lorg airson dileag a dhèanamh ri an taisbeanadh, tha na pìoban a' ruith fo na casan aca). 'S ann anns an Vom a thogas sibh uile na dealbhan anns an èideadh agaibh, far an do rinn Julie na fiolmaichean luachmhòr air cùl nan seallaidhean, fìor capsal ùine de an àm, far an dèan thu dannsa air falach bhon luchd-èisteachd ach an amharc na cloinne anns nan clasaichean agad air eagal 's gun dìochuimhnich iad ciamar a tha e a' dol. Tha an draoidheachd a tha a' dèanamh an Taigh-Cluiche sònraichte seo anns a' bhaile shònraichte seo anns an dùthaich shònrachte seo anns an àm shònra-ichte seo nas treasa anns an Vom.

Tha thu a' toirt sùil suas, agus tha thu a' faicinn gun do sgrìobh cudeigin rudeigin os cionn an trannsa, coltach ri tunail, dhan àrd-ùrlar. Tha an sgrìobhadh ag ràdh 'Oh… The Glamour of it all'.

*

Dìreach mar a tha a' mhòr-chuid de chloinn (agus deugairean, agus daoine tha mi cinnteach), b' urrainn dhomh a bhith gu math draghail mun fhèin-aithne agam. Chuir mi seachad tòrr ùine a' faireachdainn mar gun robh mi steigte eadar diofar shaoghail agus fèin-aithnean, gun a bhith comasach air gealladh a dhèanamh do aon leubail no coimhearsnachd no eile. Bha mi a' faireachdainn ro Ghàidhlig airson na cloinne Beurla – mar gun robh am blas ceàrr agam airson nan Gàidheal – gun do phòg mi cus nigheanan airson a bhith na eile-sheòrsach - da-rìribh gun do phòg mi cus bhalach airson a bhith gèidh - cha robh mi banail gu leòr airson an èididh sin - ro bhanail airson a bhith a' cluich a' gheama sin. Tha cuimhn' agam aon fheasgar gun robh mi a' rànail fhad 's a bha mi a' leughadh na h-iris *Bunty* le an lèine *Matrix* agam orm oir bha mi a' faireachdainn cho ceàrr. Cha robh mi ag iarraidh ach a bhith comasach air a dhol a-steach gu sgiobalta ann am bogsa le leubail cheart agus a bhith a' faireachdainn math mu dheidhinn, ach feuch nach fheumainn roghainn a dhèanamh no caoinidh mi.

Tha fhios agam a-nis nas sine na tha mi gu bheil coltas gòrach air seo. Ach cha robh MJ òg ach airson buntainn. Aig CYT bha mi, bha mi a' buntainn don Taigh-Cluiche am measg nan craobhan sin agus am buidheann de neòna-ichean a bha a' ruith a-steach gach oidhche Mhàirt agus Ardaoin mar ghaothan-cuairtean. Cha robh dragh orm mu dheidhinn sgoil, no dachaigh, no cò bu chòir dhomh a bhith gach là. Bha dat sam bith ceàrr na mo phearsan-tachd air chall anns a' chuan làn deugairean nas annasaich na mise, mo ghaol orra uile, agus co-dhiù carson a bhiodh na teachdan-gearra pearsantachd agam gu diofar nuair a b' urrainn dhut a bhith nad bhana-bhuidse, no neach-claid-heamh, no dìlleachdan, no maighstir an siorcais? Feuch rudeigin eile a-màireach, chan eil freagairtean ceàrr ann, agus tha thu treun airson fheuchainn.

Mar inbheach, chan eil dragh orm mu dheidhinn a dhol a-steach gu sgiobalta ann am bogsa, air sgàth 's gu bheil mi eòlach orm fhèin gus fios a bhith agam gu bheil mi leam-leat agus gum bi mi ag atharrachadh m' inntinn gu tric. B' àbhaist dhan leubail Bi a' còrdadh rium, ach a-nis tha mi nas cofhurtail le Cuèir/Queer. B' àbhaist dhomh a ràdh gun robh mi nam actress, agus an uair sin bha gràin agam air an fhacal sin, bha mi nam actar gun teagamh, ach fuirichibh, tha actress a' còrdadh rium a-ri-thist. Leis an sin, a-nis chan eil mi ach a' feuchainn ri pàirt a ghabhail ann an coimhearsnachdan a tha a saoibhreachadh m' anam. Tha mi coma dè an leubail tha thu a' cleachdadh air mo shon, bidh e ag atharrachadh a-màireach co-dhiù.

Fad mo bheatha cha b' urrainn dhomh a-riamh làn ghealladh a thoirt do rud sam bith ach dà rud: fraochan a th' agam airson tèatar agus ag innse sgeulachdan, agus am balach anns an lèine Wolverine. Chaidh an dà chuid a thoirt dhomh leis a' choimhearsnachd aig Taigh-Cluiche Chomar nan Allt.

*

Tha a' chuairt air tighinn gu crich. Tha thusa agus am balach ann an lèine Wolverine a' toirt ceum a-mach air an àrd-ùrlar agus tha e trang a-nis, loma-làn hòrmanan agus an còmhradh sgriosail aig sàr-òigridh Chomar Nan Allt. Tha an stiùiriche a' feuchainn ris a h-uile duine a chruinneachadh ann an cearcall airson geama blàth-achaidh, airson ainmean chàich ionnsachadh. Tha seo gu bhith cudromach, bidh tu airson feadhainn de na h-ainmean seo a chuimhneachadh airson a' chòrr de do bheatha.

Tha thu ag èisteachd gu dlùth gus ciamar a tha an

geama seo ag obair, chan eil thu airson mearachd a dhèanamh, 's a' toirt sgot do dhaoine gu bheil thu trì miosan ro òg airson a bhith an seo. Mar a thachras e, tha thu air an geama seo a chluich roimhe, agus leis na reflexes air leth agad bho bhliadhnaichean a chur seachad a' cluich Nintendo, chan eil dragh ort gum bi thu air seotadh le gunnaichean-meòir a-nochd.

Fhad 's a tha thu ag èisteachd airson d' ainm agus na h-ainmean aig an dithis ri do thaobh (Rachel, Caitlin), tha thu a' sgrùdadh a' bhuidhinn tro sgleò sholais an Taigh-Cluiche agus a' beachdachadh air an àite cho-roinnte seo.

Bidh an ùine agad le na daoine seo neo-chothromach ro ghoirid. A dh'aithghearr, thig an This-Here-Now gu bhith na That-There-Then. Ann am bliadhna, thèid sibh gu Manchester còmhla gus taisbeanadh a dhèanamh aig an fhèis Contacting The World, far an coinnich thu ri Tèataran Òigridh à Siria, Bangladesh, Pagastàn, Nigeria. Bidh am fèin-fhiosrachadh seo ag atharrachadh na doigh a tha thu a' faicinn an t-saoghail agus na h-ealain, agus pògaidh tu cuideigin a Iòrdan agus bidh thu daonnan a' dìochuimhneachadh an ainm aca fhad 's a tha iad ag innse dhut gu bheil iad a' dol airson tatù d' ainm fhaighinn mus fhalbh thu dhachaigh air a' phlèana. Ann an dà bliadhna, bidh tu a' suirghe air fear ro shean agus ro cheàrr, agus nuair a thig an t-àm agaibh sgaradh, feumaidh tu dùr-choimhead sìos dorchadas an Vom agus èisteachd ri monolog a sgrìobh e mu dheidhinn dè cho olc 's a tha boireannaich uile (thusa), agus gu bheil gaol ri lorg nad mhionaichean. Ann an trì bliadhna bidh tu air an Tèatar Òigridh fhàgail gus Actadh a dhèanamh aig an oilthigh agus bidh am balach àrd, caol le falt bàn a dh'fhosgail na dorsan dhut air falbh. Bliadhna às dèidh sin, tillidh sibh uile le neòinean-grèine gus cuimhneachadh air.

Agus an uair sin, beatha slàn de bharrachd. Bidh tu ag atharrachadh. Fàsaidh tu. Bidh gràdh agad. Bidh tu nad dick uaireannan. Nì thu fuck ups cuideachd. Feuchaidh tu leubailean eadar-dhealaichte ort fhèin, agus gan cruinneachadh no an tilgeil às mar a thogras tu. An rud as cudromaiche, bheir thu cead dhut fhèin a bhith uabhasach air na rudan a tha thu ag iarraidh fheuchainn gun eagal. Gheibh thu eòlas air a leithid de thoileachas agus iongnadh agus fearg is pribhleid, agus bidh thu gad stiùireadh fhèin troimhe le taing dha na h-eòlasan agus na daoine ris an do choinnich thu aig Taigh-Cluiche Chomar Nan Allt.

Ann am fichead sa h-aon bliadhna, bidh tu a' sgrìobhadh seo le gàire, air leth taingeil airson an Taigh-Cluiche ionadail am measg nan craobhan a thug a-steach thu.

*

Tha togalach ùr aig Taigh-Cluiche Chomar nan Allt a-nis. Tha e na sheasamh mu mhìle shìos an rathad bhon t-seann làraich, ceangailte ri Àrd-Sgoil Chomar Nan Allt. Dh'fhosgail an togalach ùr anns an Dàmhair 2021 agus tha e a' tabhann dha muinntir a' bhaile dà dhiofar Talla-Cluiche airson taisbeanaidhean a choimhead, agus cuideachd stiùideo dannsa agus taigh-dhealbh. Cho fada 's a tha mi air a bhith beò, cha robh taigh-dhealbh ri fhaighinn ann an Comar Nan Allt airson an 50,000 neach-fuirich.

Ged a dh'fhaodadh gu tric dìth caractar is spiorad a bhith aig togalaichean ùra, tha mi a' smaoineachadh gu bheil anam agus feallsanachd an t-seann togalaich ann fhathast, airson iadsan a tha deònach coimhead. Tha mi làn dòchais gu bheil nighean ann an-dràsta, ag ionnsachadh mu i fhèin agus a' tuiteam ann an gaol agus ag obrachadh a-mach nan leubailean a tha ceart dhi, agus tha mi an dòchas gum bi Taigh-Cluiche Chomar nan Allt ann dhi fhad 's a tha i a' toirt ceum a-mach dhan t-saoghal.

Anns an Dàmhair 2024, chaidh mi fhìn agus am balach anns an lèine Wolverine air ais gus cèilidh a chur air dòigh san t-seann togalach. Tha an t-àite far an robh an t-ionad-èisteachd, an Vom, an Jaffa Cake naomh, an staidhre thathaichte, a-nis dìreach nam fearann fàs, falamh. Tha flùraichean-fiadhaich a' fàs air an talamh. Tha na taighean-tuathanais a tha air fhàgail eadar an dual carriageway agus am pàirc-chàraichean. Tha na taighean-tuathanais sin air seasamh airson 250 bliadhna, agus nuair a strìochdas iad gu ùine agus crìonadh mu dheireadh thall, tha mi an dòchas gum fàs flùraichean-fiadhaich an sin cuideachd.

A Subtractive Process

CJ MAHONY

I don't know why I started to dig the hole.

The shovel rang as it cut through the earth, metal catching rocks. My breath revealed itself as I puffed. My cheeks were flushed from the exertion, but the movement felt good as I repeatedly slammed the shovel into the ground.

Dirt crept over the top of my falling-down socks, working its way between the fabric and my skin until it was under the soles of my feet. It is irritating to have soil in your socks. I considered pausing to reorganise myself but my trainers had become embedded in the soil. As I dug deeper, they sank further, and I did not want to lose momentum.

I remember the tearing of the skin on the inside of my soft, child hands. The raw open patches sting as they rub against the grey grain of the shovel handle. It is too big for me, but that only makes me feel stronger.

This act of revealing, or creating, a hole is also a submerging. Parts of my body are sinking. The Velcro fixings on my trainers clog up with soil. The further I dig, the more I feel encouraged to keep on hacking at the ground. How big a hole can I dig for myself?

*

1993.

I prize out the fresh, untouched forms from their plastic shells the moment the plaster has set. I sit them on my knee and appreciate their shiny surfaces. And then I carve into these still-drying lumps with no plan, just an obsessive need to do. As a result of my impatience the objects often crumble in my hands. My lap fills with broken bits.

I fill too many vessels at once. Mixing, pouring, working against the material's time. I am enthralled by the change, trying to catch the exact moment at which the flowing liquid hardens into an object.

I'm too young to buy tools, so I acquire them without permission. An old kitchen knife or a flat-head screwdriver. Hacksaw blades, the ends wrapped in tape to stop them from biting my as yet unhardened fingertips. My attempts, hurried, yet to understand the process of carving, result in larger fragments than intended. The breaks are appealing in their binaries – a mix of clean, flat planes informed by a tool and rough organic splits where the material wins.

Sometimes I am sawing simply to admire the rust of the hacksaw streaking orange lines through the pristine white plaster. Sometimes I crush the lumps with my hands. Chalky fingertips digging into the surface. Sometimes I throw the lumps against the garage wall and stamp the forms into the concrete floor, my powdered footsteps visible as I walk away.

Containers are anything I can take from the house. Tupperware, ice cream tubs, yogurt pots, beach buckets. The plaster puffs white dust from the edge of the sack as

I lug it into the garage, my young teenage body strong, satisfied with the ease, not needing assistance. Enjoying the unobserved space where I can exert myself upon objects of my own making.

1995.

I am in a field on my cousin's farm in East Lothian. My boots are caked in the wet, dark soil. They hold me firmly to the ground, yet render me unbalanced as I try to move. I attempt to keep up with the line of other bodies working. Their collective agility and pace far exceed mine. I am clumsy in the feet and in the hands, which are cold, red and muddy. I pause to straighten. In my left hand, a knife. In my right, a cabbage hanging like a decapitated head.

I am drowned in overalls. I throw the cabbage into the basket, bend back into position, move on. Slash through the base. Cut down the outer leaves. I get shouted at for taking too long. A tower of a man walks down the row towards me. I stay hunched over, work faster.

'You're not bad for a young lad, but you're cutting them too high, and …' I don't hear the instruction that follows as I fixate on those first few words. I watch and nod silently in acknowledgement. I wonder if he sees the blush rush up from the collar of my boiler suit, flooding my face.

Not bad for a young lad.

2003.

I run in the dark.
Through fields.
So early the sun isn't even close to rising.
The cold air cuts my cheeks.
The same route repeated until tree roots don't trip me.
Familiar, until
I run into the side of a horse.
A black horse.
It hadn't been there before.
Obviously.
Perhaps it was sleeping.
I hope it heard me just before the impact, had a moment to prepare.
My face turned at the last second, suddenly understanding that the horse-shaped mass was a different sort of darkness.
I narrowly avoid breaking my nose.
I fall over backwards.
The horse runs off, and so do I.

This desire to move dangerously through the dark continues when I move to the city.

It is always the same, the running, in the murkiness of the pre-morning. Other people horrified by the risks. But I am compelled by the feeling of being hidden, my movement unobserved, disembodied by the darkness.

On those early mornings I observe many moments in other people's lives. The end of their days at the start of mine. I see fighting couples. Observe weaving drunks. A dead body being covered by a tarpaulin. An unconscious person about to catch fire. I put out the fire. I keep running.

1986.

  'Call me Max.'

Or was it Sam?

They called me a tomboy, referred to it as a phase. I wonder what it would be seen as now, what concern it would cause.

There was frustration at the neglect of a name I was not willing to use, mixed with exhaustion after the shouting fits and raging rows over clothing.

  'But Catriona is such a beautiful name.'

It is, for someone.

2023.

Four weeks ago, you got in the shower with me so you could assist with my first full wash. Your naked body opposite mine. You soaked the adhesive strips that covered my incisions. You gently passed a flannel across my body, drawing soapy lines over me as I wept. You wiped away the two week old room full of strangers.

At home you sat with candles burning for the duration of my suspended time. Trying not to be felled by the fear that I might die in some tragic medical accident on an operating table with my arms outstretched.

I step out of the shower, and you wrap me in a large, soft towel. I am aware that our height discrepancy means you are working on your tiptoes. In our bedroom you gently move me this way and that as you remove my surgical tape carefully. I lean on your shoulder while you help me into my pants.

A friend said they could share information about living with someone who is transitioning. My immediate thought was, I'm not transitioning, I am involved in a subtractive process. An adjustment of a body that is wrangling with its parts. In this balancing act I am as troubled by them as I am by any other gendering part of my body, aware that as I carve away at one part, I highlight another. This process is about redefining my outline.

I come to realise that I am fighting myself. Seeking release from gendered assumptions. From the weight of what might be other people's thoughts and opinions of my body, both before and after my surgery. I contemplate the non-binary bodies I see on social media that I do not replicate. I am both too old and have not been binary enough in my non-binary transformation.

We stand in the kitchen. You have the scales out and you are pouring yellow dried lentils into two plastic bags. When you have finished you hold the masses aloft. They hang between us. I appreciate the choice of lentils looking like little fat cells. We admire the masses, these presences that are now absences. They feel like tangible subtractions to contemplate once I'm back on the sofa.

Where is gender? We recognise people through movement. What gender is my movement? Could I move differently? Do I not want to be recognised? What goes into the unconscious calculation of pattern recognition? Can it be unbalanced by my subtractive process?

I slept upright on the sofa for the first few nights because I was so worried about failing at back sleeping, and in my sleepless haze I contemplated how, if someone broke in through the front door that I was sleeping by, I would be unable to protect you.

When I go outside for my slow recovery walks, I think about you caring for me. I consider how we will carry on caring for one another, as our bodies age, supporting each other with our ever-changing outlines.

*

I return to the hole and throw myself in – she hits the bottom of the hole with a rubbery thud. That other me lies there in the mud, sinks in a little, the weight of her body pressing down. I contemplate that body.

I wonder if the hole is a manifestation of my battle with my queerness, an attempt to deal with the homophobia I absorbed. Is that why I was so intent on digging it? A deep hole for all the things that I wanted to dispose of? I pull her back up. Below, the imprint of her body remains.

I think about the dialogue I would write for the actors in a crime drama. Maybe a group of forensic pathologists standing around the top of the hole looking down. Considering the outline. What deductions would they make from the imprint her body made? Would they fill it with plaster like a footprint? I am briefly horrified at the prospect of the negative made positive in plaster. I think of my rust-covered tools.

2025.

If I need a place, can it be the subtractive place of sculpture?

This place I continually re-make for myself, so I can inhabit it.

By its nature, sculpture is either an additive or a subtractive process. The additive process builds up, layers, models to achieve the intended shape. The subtractive process removes material, taking it away to reveal the desired form. I was never drawn to the additive process, finding it too full and unwieldy, too much uncertainty in the adornment.

I preferred subtraction. But sculpture is always a question of knowing when to stop. How do you know when you've added enough, or taken away too much, and lost the balance?

As I think about my identity – the place of it – I think about what I am making now and I am struck with the circular nature of practice. At art school I forced my body to leave impressions in clay. It was a private process, full of brutality. A physical exchange. I punched the surface, dug with my fingertips. Then I filled these voids with plaster, so I could excavate the bone-like stretches of fragmented body.

Now, I force impressions into the surface of other materials. The exchange is still a physical one. The brutality remains. But this time there is also a moment of holding, when the material is in its most precarious state. Cracks run through it. I work with the vulnerability, bringing it to the surface.

The objects I make are damaged but they are also filled with resilience. They crumble each time they are handled but in that process they change, evolve. The marks in the surface are a confluence of forces. Reminders of a critical point of transformation.

Difficult to identify purely based on an outline.

I see the works as object bodies. Abstractions. When they greet you in a gallery the object body is across from you. Hung around the height of my torso, it invites you to think of your body, of being bodily. Your life lived, the fragility of health. Your ageing. Your own changes. The impression you leave behind.

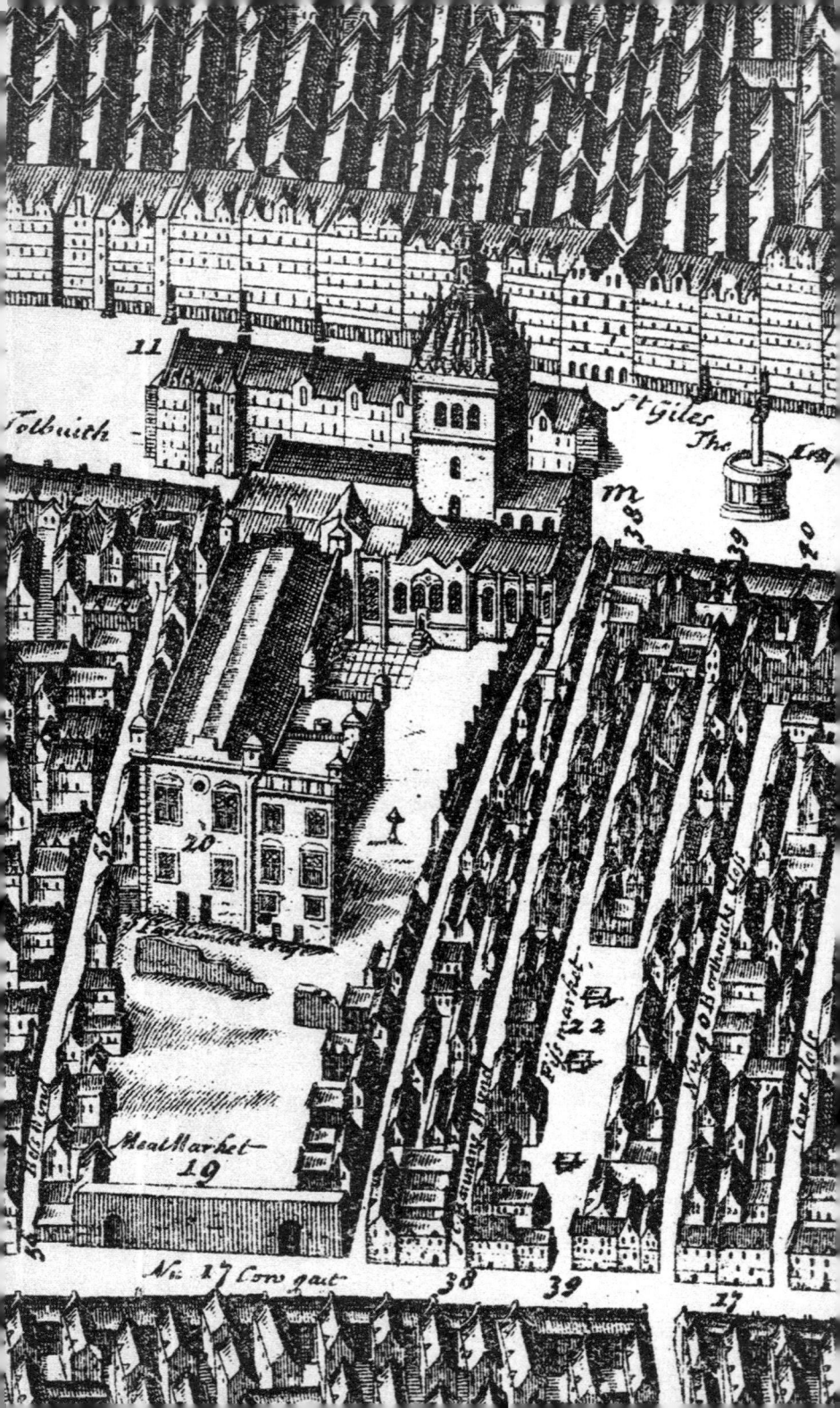

11

Tolbuith

St Giles
The La..

38

39
40

m

36

20

Parliament ..

Land O Bothwick

Court Close

39

Fish market
22

Meal Market
19

No. 17 Cow gait

38   39   17

My Sapphic City

ASHLEY DOUGLAS

The long green strip of Princes Street Gardens, hemmed in by grand shopfronts and the railway line linking Haymarket and Waverley stations, may appear to be the very heart of the traditional Edinburgh cityscape. But just as the pristine gardens once replaced the marshy Nor Loch, there is more to their recent history than can be seen at first glance. Only four days after the introduction of Section 28 in 1988, Princes Street Gardens had played host to the largest and highest profile LGBTQ+ protest event Scotland had ever seen. The anti-gay censorship clause had been in force for less than a week when the capital's queer community and allies rallied to make their disgust clear. In open defiance of the clause, which specifically prohibited local authorities from 'promoting homosexuality', Edinburgh's council[1] awarded the organising group a grant to help run the event. The amount involved was small, a couple of hundred pounds, but the symbolic statement was huge. Lark in the Park, as the protest was known, was restaged in 1989 and 1992 – the year I was born in Edinburgh.

In the summer of 1995, my city – which had so swiftly galvanised to oppose Section 28 – was the stage for the first major Pride march in Scotland. Bolstered by an official stamp of approval from the council, the march

1   In 1996, the current City of Edinburgh Council replaced both the City of Edinburgh District Council (the body that awarded the funding grant to Lark in the Park) and the Lothian Regional Council (which approved the 1995 Pride March).

assembled at Broughton Place, not far from where I would attend primary school. An estimated 3,000 people, more than expected, lit up Edinburgh in love, solidarity and anger that day, claiming the streets as their own.[2] They marched along Princes Street and up the Mound before continuing along George IV Bridge, where the historic day culminated with a festival in the Meadows[3] – a stone's throw from the maternity hospital where I'd entered the world.

In 1999, when I was a school pupil, Scotland's devolved Parliament was established. Until the parliament building at Holyrood was completed in 2004, it met in the Assembly Hall of the Church of Scotland. The first Pride marchers had passed under its domineering glare in 1995 as they looped round the Mound. It was in that unlikely space, with John Knox glowering in the courtyard outside, that one of the new Parliament's very first acts, in 2000, was to wipe Section 28 off the statute books in Scotland (albeit not without vitriolic opposition). From the later 2000s onwards, by then firmly ensconced at the foot of the Royal Mile opposite Holyrood Palace, the Scottish Parliament enacted a series of laws in relation to LGBTQ+ equality, from equal adoption rights – which finally came into force in 2009 – to equal marriage, in 2014.

Not that I knew any of this at the time – the times when it would have mattered most.

*

2   With sincere thanks to Tim Hopkins, who was part of the group that organised the original Lark in the Park in 1988 and co-ordinator of the 1995 Pride March, for his generous sharing of recollections and material. Thanks also to Damian Barr for sharing his recollections of the Pride March.

3   The full route of the 1995 Pride March was as follows: Broughton Street, Leith Street, Princes Street, the Mound, North Bank Street, Bank Street, George IV Bridge, Bristo Place, Teviot Place, and down Middle Meadow Walk to the Meadows.

I wasn't taken to the 1995 march. I wasn't born into that sort of household. I had the worst sort of start in life you could imagine for a child. It was so bad I often wished I hadn't been born at all; so bad I still wish that today, sometimes, despite all the love and happiness I've found. This is not the place to share details of my childhood. Suffice to say that there was no support to be found in the 'home' for a young gay me, or any other part of me. 'Home' was not a safe haven, but a place of danger; when I was just 16, I fled it altogether.

School was, in many ways, my refuge – but not for the part of me that was gay. Section 28 was still in force while I was at primary school, and its legacy lived on during my high school years in the 2000s.[4] LGBTQ+ people, past or present, did not meaningfully appear in any lesson – let alone being taught that it was okay to be gay. It was as if queer people didn't exist, and never had. I had no positive representations of gay relationships – to the contrary, all I knew was that 'gay', 'poof' and 'dyke' were slurs: bad things that you definitely didn't want to be. In the long shadow cast by Section 28, school did nothing to counter those (and worse) words and sentiments, which I absorbed, unmitigated, throughout my youth. Homophobia, explicit and insidious, polluted the societal water I was swimming in.

In 2010, after fleeing 'home', I made it to my first safe haven, university in St Andrews, through the support of the Sutton Trust summer school and my high school. I

---

4   Fortunately, things are better for LGBTQ+ pupils in Scottish state schools today. In 2021, as a result of the Time for Inclusive Education (TIE) campaign (co-founded by Jordan Daly and Liam Stevenson), Scotland became the first country in the world to embed LGBTQ+ inclusive education across the curriculum. I was honoured to work with TIE on lesson plans focusing on Marie Maitland, which formed part of the launch of inclusive education in 2021, and continue to work with TIE on new resources. Together, we also commissioned an imagined portrait of Marie, which is now on display in the Scottish National Portrait Gallery, as well as featuring in the schools resources.

graduated in 2014, the year that equal marriage passed into law in Scotland – and yet I have no recollection of that event. It simply can't have registered as relevant to me. Even in my 20s, when I thought of marriage, I thought of a man and a woman; of *me* and a man. I could not *imagine* being married to a woman. The internalised homophobia, the compulsory heterosexuality, was so painfully strong.

I went on to study a master's degree in Scottish History – but I wasn't about to learn anything about my queer ancestors in the history department of Scotland's oldest university. The 1603 Union of Crowns and the 1707 Union of Parliaments loomed large on the curriculum. We studied each in great political, religious and economic detail. But there was no hint that both of the monarchs associated with those momentous events, King James VI & I and Queen Anne respectively, were also significant figures of queer history – or of any other aspect of Scotland's LGBTQ+ history. Just like at school, it was as if no such thing existed.

Discovering my queer self, and my queer history, would take another few years. It would involve a series of happy accidents – and a return to the city of my birth.

*

In 2016, when I was 23 and in the middle of my history postgraduate degree, my life was transformed. I met and fell in love with the woman who is now my wife, Eilidh, in Edinburgh. Nothing had ever felt so right or true – the force of my feelings for her, our love for one another, swept away all my hesitations and discomfort about 'liking women' overnight. If *this* was being gay, then I couldn't deny it any longer – didn't want to deny it any longer. In a matter of months, I went from unsure and ashamed, to scream-it-from-the-rooftops levels of proudly engaged to a woman. We got married the very next year. Finally, I was out – but it took falling in love with and marrying a woman to get there. I had never been confident enough to be my full and true self before I met Eilidh. For me, embracing being a queer woman is inextricable from falling in love with her. I came to recognise and love myself as a queer woman through loving, and being loved by, her.

Eilidh's journey was different to mine. Although still far from easy, she had embraced her lesbian identity much earlier and with more confidence. However, when it came to role models, or historical precedents, she had about as little to go on as I did – as far as she was aware, lesbian history meaningfully started with *The L Word* in 2004, and the fictional couple of Bette and Tina embodied the most realistic representation of a relationship between women she could hope for.

In 2017, when Eilidh and I got married at Falkland Palace (a favoured retreat of Mary, Queen of Scots), one of our readings was 1 Corinthians 13, from *The New Testament in Scots*: that timeless and moving bible passage about love, translated into the historical language of state, including: 'Luve is patientfu; luve is couthie an kind; luve is naither jailous, nor vauntie wi pride; it's no self seekin, it's no misleared, it's no easy roozed'.[5] It was beautiful, but it is a source of enduring regret that we had no idea, at that point, that we could have had a reading of a breathtaking lesbian love poem, whose author drew on biblical scripture to exalt her love for another woman, at a time

5 *The New Testament in Scots*, translated by W L Lorimer, Edinburgh: Canongate, 2012 [1983]

when Scots was still the language of the kingdom, more than four hundred years ago. At the time of our wedding, we had never even heard of Marie Maitland – the historical lesbian poet whose significance to not just Scottish, but global, queer history can scarcely be overstated, and whose biography, nearly a decade on, I find myself writing.

Marie lived from c1546 to 1596. A contemporary of Mary, Queen of Scots and John Knox, she was born into the influential Maitland of Lethington family – her brothers, in particular, dominated Scottish politics during this era.[6] In 1561, in the twist of fate that changed everything, Marie's father, the judge and poet Sir Richard Maitland of Lethington, went entirely blind. The youngest daughter, and the only one still unmarried and at home, thus it was that a teenage Marie first became her father's literary and legal secretary – a role in which she would serve for the next 25 years. In a life path very different to that of her three sisters, who had all been promptly married off, Marie remained abnormally unwed for most of her adult life. This gave her the relative freedom to pursue her own learning and writing – and to fall in love with another woman, which we know about because she immortalised that love in poetry, recorded surreptitiously, but still dangerously, still bravely, in a manuscript ostensibly of her father's poetry.

The Scottish Reformation of 1560 heralded an era in which Scotland was suffocated by a particularly extreme, virulently misogynist brand of Calvinism, where women were deemed inferior to men in every way, and where 'sodomy' (whether between two men or two women) was

6   Marie's father, Sir Richard, was a judge, privy counsellor and Keeper of the Great Seal under Mary, Queen of Scots; her brother William was Secretary to Mary, Queen of Scots (Secretary Lethington); her brother John was later Chancellor to her son, King James VI (Chancellor Maitland).

one of the worst transgressions imaginable.[7] And yet it was in that unthinkably hostile climate of immediately post-Reformation Scotland that Marie declared to her female love, with unmissable eroticism, '*Ye wield me holie [wholly] at your will and raviss [ravish] my affectioun*'– and that, later in the same poem, she stated her unequivocal desire to *marry* the woman that she loved. Marie invoked Ruth's pledge of ever-lasting devotion to Naomi in the Old Testament and wrote that, if only she and her lover could '*with joyfull hairt*' be married, they would not be the two '*unhappie wemen*' that they were. Of course, in the 1500s, there could be no realistic hope or prospect of them ever actually being able to marry. But in their hearts, Marie stated, '*nocht but deid [nothing but death]*' could ever divorce them: their love, she vowed, would prove that '*thair is mair constancie in our sex, than ever amang men has been*'.

This poem appears in a manuscript that Marie completed in 1586, along with a series of other technically anonymous, but female-authored, poems, slipped in among the many pages of authoritative male-authored verse. Marie's name is emblazoned on the manuscript's title page, twice. Various poems within its pages confirm her authorship, and her reputation as a poet. In one poem, Marie is even named as a poetic heir to Sappho of Lesbos – the ancient Greek poet who wrote explicit poetry about her love for women, and gave us the very words 'sapphic' and 'lesbian'. Indeed, Marie is one of the earliest known authors of explicitly lesbian poetry in Europe since Sappho herself, making her a key figure in

---

7 In 1570, for example, two men were convicted of 'sodomy' and executed in Edinburgh. In 1625, in Glasgow, two women were found guilty of 'sodomy', publicly condemned, and sentenced to separate from each other on pain of excommunication. Numerous other individuals in this period, male and female, were tried for sodomy and witchcraft; the two charges were viewed as inextricable and were often conflated.

the history of women who love women.

And Edinburgh was her city – our city was her city! Marie spent significant chunks of her life in the capital. Many original surviving documents relating to Marie announce that she signed her name to them '*At Edinburgh*'. We also know that Marie, who lived a unique life as a woman in early modern Scotland in many ways, often appeared before the Court of Session, which was housed in St Giles Cathedral. Here, Marie would astutely protect her legal and financial interests by, for example, submitting signed contracts to be authoritatively, centrally recorded. One such record, mentioning her by name, begins as follows:

> '*In presens of the lordis of counsale comperat person-alie ... Marie Maitland ... and gave in this contract ... and desyreit the samyn to be insyrt and registrat in the buikis of counsale*'.[8]

Further down the High Street from where she did her court business at St Giles was the townhouse in which Marie resided during the latter part of her life. This home was said to be '*lyand withein the burght of edinburgh on the north syde of the streit thairof foiranenttis the salt trone*' – or 'opposite the salt tron', the burgh's large weighing beams ('tron') for measuring salt.[9] Today, that places it across from the tellingly named Tron Kirk, its appellation testifying to the important salt tron that stood outside it for centuries. It's tricky to pinpoint the exact spot where Marie's building stood, but it must have been somewhere

8 Translation: 'In the presence of the Lords of Council [ie before the court] appeared personally ... Marie Maitland ... and gave in this contract ... and desired the same to be inserted and registered in the books of council'.

9 Translation: 'located within the burgh of Edinburgh on the north side of the street thereof opposite the salt tron'.

amidst the short row of buildings facing the modern kirk, truncated by North Bridge to the east and Cockburn Street to the west (now occupied at ground level by a tourist shop selling cashmere, tartan and tweeds, and a branch of the chain restaurant Bella Italia). In any event, when I, or any other local or visitor, walk the stretch of the High Street between St Giles and the Tron today, we are walking in the footsteps of Scotland's sixteenth-century Sappho, and in the direct vicinity of the townhouse in which she once dwelt.

Despite the punishingly puritanical society that she lived in, Marie believed with all her heart and soul in the validity, equality and righteousness of the love between her and another woman. If the ghost of Marie looked out of her Edinburgh townhouse window in June today, more than four hundred years since she walked the city's streets, she would be stunned to see thousands upon thousands of proud and open queer people and their allies streaming past, faces painted with rainbows and sparkling with glitter, waving flags and holding up placards with unabashedly bold messages of love and defiance, as Edinburgh's Pride march makes its way up the High Street from Holyrood. She would see wives – like me and Eilidh! – walking hand in hand, legally married, kissing in broad daylight; she might even spot someone dressed as Sappho. She would scarcely believe her eyes. She would, I am certain, love it.

*

Not that Eilidh or I could possibly have known any of this, back when we first met. Over the past few years, I have been undertaking painstaking original archival research into Marie's life. The snippets above are just some of what I have unearthed, shared here for the very first time. When the biography of Marie that I am currently writing is published, it will be – despite her significance, despite all the surviving records relating to her – the first book ever written about her.

I first stumbled upon Marie's poetry, by chance, while researching something else. Immediately recognising, hardly believing, its significance – among the earliest known lesbian love poetry in all of Europe since Sappho herself, written in post-Reformation Scotland! – I began to share it, as widely as possible. Before that point, Marie was virtually unknown: a case study of how the evidence for women's, and especially queer women's, history is so often ignored and undermined.[10] I have lost count of the number of queer women who have recently come across my work on Marie, or attended an event I've spoken at, and exclaimed to me afterwards, 'I cannot believe I didn't know about her before!' – their excitement mixed with confusion, and even embarrassment. But of course they didn't know about her, because you can't know what you're not told about.

Sharing the significance of Marie's sapphic poetry, and then taking it upon myself to research her wider story, has become a major focus of my life over the past half-decade. On one level, it is a privilege, and hugely exciting, to have been able to uncover so much material, unseen – figuratively in some cases, literally in others – for centuries; to be the person reconstructing and sharing Marie's amazing story. At the same time, I can't help but feel sad and angry that it has been left to me, a queer woman, to meaningfully recognise and share the lesbian and female-authored poetry in the pages of Marie's manu-

---

10   I first published an article about Marie's most powerful lesbian love poem with the National Library of Scotland for LGBTQ+ History Month in February 2021.

script – *and* to go looking for the wider evidence of the life she lived. Although, thankfully, I have the requisite historical training through my university degrees, this is work done around my main job. After all, if I don't tell Marie's story, who will? Nobody has ever deemed her life worthy of research before.

So it is that, over the past years, I have hunted out the traces of Marie's life in the Edinburgh of centuries past, in the archival institutions of modern Edinburgh that have diligently preserved the records, waiting for the right person to come and seek their secrets. I have lost count of the number of times I have walked down North Bridge, passing Marie's townhouse on my left, on my way to the grand eighteenth-century edifice of HM General Register House. There, I have spent many hours (many of them fruitless!) in the historical search room, trawling through volume upon volume of untranscribed records from the 1500s, just in case – maybe, hopefully – there was something relevant to Marie to be found. I have also long since lost track of how many a Saturday I have spent ensconced in the National Library of Scotland on George IV Bridge, the proud crown steeple of St Giles and the looming mass of Arthur's Seat dominating the view from special collections on the top floor, just as they dominated the skyline of Marie's Edinburgh. In these hushed environs of the nation's main historical archives, I have wept, once or twice, as my eyes, after hours of discouraging nothing, finally alighted on an unmistakable 'Maitland' – the first glimpse of another surviving document that would enrich my understanding of Marie. On other occasions, I have had to refrain from punching the air and whooping out loud, as certain manuscripts, patiently sourced and carefully scrutinised, have finally revealed their transformational secrets.

*

Edinburgh is part of me and I am part of it. The city is one of the most meaningful, constant and rooting presences in my life. It's where I was born, the city whose streets I've walked as long as I can remember. It's also the place I've built my adult life, with my wife, today. As I've learnt more about Edinburgh's queer history – *my* history – in just the past months and years, I've begun to feel even more connected to the city of my birth, and even more secure in my queer identity. I am not just a proud queer woman, but a proud queer woman *of Edinburgh*. Two facts of which I am proud: I was born in Edinburgh and I was born gay.

I only wish I'd known my city's queer history sooner, and that I hadn't had to search it all out, or stumble upon it, myself. Everything I have learned about Marie's life, including her strong Edinburgh connections, I have had to find out for myself, through scrupulous research over years, having first happened upon her poetry by chance. The first I knew that 2025 marked the 30th anniversary of Scotland's first Pride, let alone that it took place in Edinburgh, was when I was approached to contribute to this book. Likewise, I knew nothing of the Lark in the Park protests until I began researching for this chapter.

When I walk through Princes Street Gardens now, I think of the hundreds of wearied but defiant souls who gathered there, including in the very year that I was born, trying to make the world a better and safer place for me to grow up in. When I walk through the Meadows, I think of the historic festival that took place there in 1995, when thousands gathered to celebrate a part of me that I would spend so many years hating and hiding. I'm grateful I know this now; I wish I'd known before.

When I look up at Arthur's Seat today, I smile as I think about the time that Eilidh and I climbed it in the predawn darkness, not long after we first met, to watch the sun rise over the city — *and* about how Marie's sixteenth-century eyes would have taken in the exact same hulk of ancient volcano and craggy cliffs. I can't walk the High Street without thinking about Marie, a woman who exhibited inspirational levels of bravery and love for herself, as a woman who loved other women, in the utterly uncomprehending and hateful environment of 1500s Scotland. I feel connected, as a queer woman, to my sapphic ancestors, as solidly as the volcanic rock the city is built upon. I draw comfort and strength from them now; I only wish I'd been able to before.

How different my story, as a queer woman at least, might have been, if I'd been presented with evidence of my city's queer history, my history, in its built environment. How much sooner might I have come to find and love myself if I'd seen, with the vulnerable, searching eyes of one of my younger selves, a statue of Marie Maitland (just imagine!) – or even just a humble plaque honouring her – by St Giles Cathedral or the Tron Kirk. But any opportunity to find strength or comfort in my city's queer history, to see myself reflected back in the world around me, was denied me by its silence; and it is a silence that continues to this day.

At the sites of Scotland's Stonewall moments, the city is so quiet you could hear a protest pin drop. Nothing in Princes Street Gardens memorialises the brave hundreds who gathered to protest Section 28 within days of its coming into force, or the civil disobedience of the council that defiantly funded them. No plaque at Broughton Place tells you that it was here, in 1995, that thousands of souls assembled, too many to fit, to make history; nothing in the Meadows tells you that it was here that Scotland's first Pride march culminated in festivities. Unlike Sappho in Lesbos, and Anne Lister in Halifax, Marie has no statue in Edinburgh. The built environment of Scotland's capital boasts of its own queer icon Marie Maitland not a jot. No square in Makars Court proclaims her name along with a line from her verse. Nowhere in St Giles is there so much as a whisper that this most monumental Edinburgh building is inextricably associated with such a significant figure of LGBTQ+ history. Down by the Tron, there is no plaque in sight to tell you that 'Scotland's 16th-Century Sappho once lived near this spot'.

Edinburgh has an embarrassment of riches when it comes to recorded queer history, both recent and centuries-old. But none of it is physically commemorated. Campaigner and author of *Where are the Women?* Sara Sheridan, points out that the UK average for statues to named women (excluding royals) is a paltry 3 per cent, and that Edinburgh – where there are more statues of animals than named women – ranks even more poorly than that. When it comes to individuals and events of queer significance, the capital's failure to commemorate is even more complete: to the best of my knowledge at the time of writing, the figure is zero.

*

These days, I am joyously, openly gay. I love being a lesbian. All the best parts of my life are rooted in being a queer woman. I know myself, and I know love; I know my queer history, and I know my city's history. Nothing and nobody could ever make me feel any differently. But it took me such a long and painful time to get here. Edinburgh, my city, could have held me sooner. I so wish it had.

The Club,
4 Queens Crescent

LOUISE WELSH

'It's not what they were, dear, as much as what they were doing in the central garden.'

In winter, if I stand at my sitting room window and angle myself to the left, I can make out the roof of 4 Queens Crescent, peeking above a dense crosshatch of branches. The central garden's iron railings are roughly five feet tall, their spikes blunted. It is easy for an athletic person to punt themselves over, onto the lawn and slip into the bushes beyond. During the day it is overlooked by the Georgian houses that form a half-moon around it.

Most of the houses are converted into flats. Some are commercial premises. There is a doctor, a vet, an insurance company, the Theosophical Society in Scotland and Visibility, a centre for visually impaired people. Each window sees a different angle of trees and greenery, the long war between magpies and rooks, busy squirrels, the change of season.

In spring frothing blossom obscures some sightlines. In summer, canopies of green leaves give an illusion of privacy. But this is the centre of the city. Eyes are everywhere.

I am writing this on 10 January. It is twenty past four in the afternoon. The sun has almost set, my desk lamp is on, my window blinds up. My apartment consists of four rooms plus a small hallway and a bathroom. My office is at the back of the building. Other apartment windows stare into mine. I am visible as I type this. Small, hunched over my computer in an old jumper and sweatpants, face illuminated in the computer's glow. A blanket is tucked across my knees, and I have wrapped a tartan shawl around my shoulders. The temperature is minus one outside, set to drop, and I am cold.

I have just got up and gone to the front of my apartment to check that I really can see number 4 from the sitting room window. It was darker out there. The square empty except for a man walking away from the subway. I watched him pass beneath a streetlight and thought how lonely he looked, like a figure in an Atkinson Grimshaw painting, a silhouette, there to add perspective to the buildings.

Number 4 was lost in the shadows, the central garden a pool of black. There are private places beneath the trees but tonight is too cold for fooling around outdoors. The derelict fountain will be frosted with ice, the garden left to birds, bats, mice and voles. I heard a fox screech – I thought it was a fox – closed the shutters and returned to my desk where I sit now. A person in a pool of light.

A view from other windows.

'It's not what they were, dear, as much as what they were doing in the central garden.'

What they were, were gay men and the occasional lesbian. I knew my neighbour was sincere when she told us that it was 'not what they were' that concerned her. She had welcomed my partner Zoë and me from the moment we moved into our building. When equal marriage was being hotly debated, Cardinal Keith O'Brien and others spewing poison, sections of social media a cesspit, she had made a point of telling us, 'As far as I'm concerned, dears, Love is Love.' She was generous towards my novels too, buying them as presents for friends, regardless of the spicy same-sex encounters they sometimes detail. When she died a few years ago, in her 90s, we cried. When her apartment went up for sale, we put a bid in. We live there now.

When I look out of my sitting room window, I look out onto the view of changing seasons my neighbour saw for over 40 years. I think of her often.

I did not have to ask what the men from number 4 were doing in the central garden. It was, I assumed, what people often do after a night out at a club, alfresco houghmagandie, sylvan in the city.

Several of the trees in the central garden reach higher than the houses that surround them. How deep do their roots descend? Our district is built on coal mines, sandstone quarries and landed estates. The fountain at the centre of the pleasure garden caps an old mineshaft. I wonder about these old seams. Do they still exist, intersected by tree roots, running with water and ground dwellers? Insects and larvae? Rats?

Mines and quarries make unstable foundations, but back in the early nineteenth century Glaswegians were keen to move west and architects and builders keen to oblige. Our crescent was one of the earliest sites developed in the west of the city.[1] It was designed by John Bryce, who is also responsible for the facade of Glasgow Necropolis catacombs, erected in 1831, six years before Victoria became Queen.

The graveyard connection pleases me. The catacombs' facade is fancier than Queens Crescent. A plaque above

1 Thanks to Dr Nicole Cumming, Steven Grainger and Zoë Strachan, who all shared research with me.

the entrance declares that the Necropolis holds, 'resting places for generations yet unborn'. It gives me a funny feeling, thinking of babies, waiting in the ether (or wherever they reside) to live out their lives, always destined to be deposited in the Necropolis.

Of course I do not believe in babies waiting in the ether, or destiny, but nevertheless I see the children in my mind's eye. Plump, curly-haired cherubs, Raphael angels, elbows resting on blue clouds, eager to be born.

The poor foundations made themselves known in the 1960s, 1970s and 1980s in the form of subsidence. Some people believe that the demolition of much of the busy residential and shopping district of St George's Cross to make the M8 motorway contributed to the problem. Whatever the cause, banks and building societies became reluctant to grant mortgages on the unstable properties. Many fell into the hands of slum landlords. The area around Queens Crescent became a red-light zone. Glimpses of that period linger in the No Loitering signs painted on the entrances to some closes further up West Princes Street. Loitering being a euphemism for the kind of activity neighbours objected to in the Central Garden.

The drop in the district's fortunes enabled people to move in who would have been unable to afford the high rents and property prices the district previously commanded. These included newcomers from South India and else-where, Art School and University students, writers and artists, people like us.

Our neighbour would not have described herself as an activist, but when plans were made to make the central garden into a Park and Ride to serve St George's Cross subway station, she and other citizens vigorously opposed them. Later she was instrumental in the campaign to have the district designated a conservation zone, though if you exit the subway and enter our square, conservation zone is not the phrase that leaps to mind.

Sections of our area are still collapsing. Two blocks of Melrose Street, a continuation of Queens Crescent and the first structure you see as you step from the underpass that leads from the subway, are shuttered and derelict. In 2020 the blocks were found to be 'below tolerable standard' and taken over by the council after no registered owner was identified – though someone had been collecting rent from the people who lodged there. The buildings list towards the subway station, like an old man with a bad back. Will we wake one night to the sound of crashing sandstone, the crack and shatter of glass, explosions of dust?

Twenty years ago, two young students died in a fire in one of the basement flats in the now-abandoned buildings. Their landlord went to jail for two and a half years and was banned from renting out property. In 2019 he was fined £300 for threatening a tenant in one of the flats, demanding rent.

Buddleia sprouts from the guttering of number 4. The wrought-iron railings that enclose the drop to the basement tilt drunkenly. The windows' frames are rotting, window glass loose. Faint glimpses of its interior hint at disaster. I have spotted no face at the window, never heard its door slam and yet sometimes I think there may be someone living there, or maybe just passing through. Perhaps I am detecting memories. The stamp of Dr Marten's dancing to Bronski Beat, Frankie, Wham! and the Pet Shop Boys, Dead or Alive.

When I turn my swivel chair towards my workroom window, I see distant squares of light, other computers glowing in rooms across the back courtyard. People working from home, studying, online shopping, scrolling through social media. I wonder if any of the glimmering screens are connected to the Dark Web and if there is something wrong with me that my mind turns so readily to questions like that. Why instead of flitting around the treetops do I descend into tangled roots and abandoned mineshafts? Why can't I banish basement fires from my mind, enjoy the beauty of sprouting Buddleia? Stop conjuring ghosts?

'It's not what they were, dear, as much as what they were doing in the central garden.'

In 1919 number 4 Queens Crescent became the Regimental Club of the Seaforth Highlanders. It was part of a busy social centre. The Scottish Western Motor Club revved its engines at number 14. The Spanish Consul was located at number 15. The Clarion Cycling Club at number 6 was succeeded by the Maryhill Railway Workers' Club in the late 1950s. Number 2 Queens Crescent became the home of the Scottish National Institute for the War Blinded in 1929. Number 8 housed the Cameronian Highlanders Club.

Our square was no stranger to regimental ties. This concentration of military influence was not random. The Drill Hall further down West Princes Street (subsequently the Ballet School, which makes sense when you think about it) had been a centre for military recruitment and training since 1897. It was an early home of the Boys Brigade. First Chief Scout Lord Baden Powell was an honoured guest. The 5th Battalion of the Cameronians trained there before marching to the Western Front in 1914.

The clubs were male and strictly codified. Women (wives) in one corner, men (the blue blazer brigade) dominating the room. Camaraderie, shared interests and experience were at their heart, but they also had a practical advantage. The Licensing (Scotland) Act of 1921 restricted opening times for public houses to 11.30am–3pm and 5.30pm–10pm, with a ban on Sunday trading. Licensed private clubs were allowed to serve alcohol during dry hours, when your throat might feel like cutting itself.

The rise of feminism and counterculture combined with changes in licensing laws saw a decline in membership of military clubs. The Seaforth Highlanders Club was resident at number 4 Queens Crescent for over 50 years. When they moved out in the late 1970s another shared interest, shared experience group was ready to take their place.

'It's not what they were, dear, as much as what they were doing in the central garden.'

Homosexuality was decriminalised in Scotland in 1980, 13 years after it had been decriminalised in England. Many queer Scots took the train or bus down to London, hoping to escape rampant, state-sanctioned homophobia. Jimmy Somerville captures the necessity to flee south in the video for Bronski Beat's hi-NRG chart topper *Smalltown Boy*. Did homophobes tap their feet to *Smalltown Boy*? Did they dance to its beats? In the 1970s and 1980s, men's fashion was possibly the most flamboyant it had been since regency times. Hair was long, heels high, crotches tight, shirts patterned, jewellery abundant, moustaches bold. Straight shipyard workers strutted about dressed like Tom of Finland, unaware that their ultra manliness was aping gay fashion.

Gays were influencing music and fashion, but homo-phobia was far from niche.

Opposition to decriminalisation in Scotland was not a new thing. A *Daily Record* poll following the Wolfenden

Report in England (1957) concluded that 85 per cent of Scots were opposed to decriminalisation. With the exception of a few enlightened activists, church groups were consistently vehement in their opposition. The General Assembly of the Church of Scotland insisted that decriminalisation would 'lead to further and greater depravities'.

Guardians of the law upheld the prejudice. In 1980, the Grampian Police handbook stated, 'The terms "sodomy", "lewd and libidinous practices" etc. where used in law give little indication of the nature of these offences, the manner in which they are usually committed, and the evils they are liable to bring in their train ...'[2]

Unofficial gay bars did exist. Popular Glasgow venues included The Duke of Wellington, The Waterloo, Vintners and Tennent's Bar (seats beyond the pole). Gay men would approach and exit these establishments with caution, alert for gay bashers and muggers. Homosexuality was punishable by imprisonment. The police were less than sympathetic to gay men who complained of being beaten up and/or robbed.

It was into this hostile atmosphere that the Scottish Minorities Group (SMG) launched their campaign for the decriminalisation of homosexuality. SMG also ran gay discos in Glasgow in venues such as Partick Burgh Halls and Woodside Halls. Despite homosexuality being illegal, the licensing authority approved liquor licenses for these events.

In 1979, SMG, who had changed their name to the Scottish Homosexual Rights Group, began planning to open Scotland's very first official gay club. The closure of the Regimental Club of the Seaforth Highlanders had left

2   Anna Walker, 'Scotland leads Europe on LGBT rights, but shouldn't forget its past', 10 December 2015, theconversation.com/scotland-leads-europe-on-lgbt-rights-but-shouldnt-forget-its-past-51420, accessed 10 February 2025

number 4 empty. Scottish Homosexual Rights Group raised the £56,000 necessary to secure the premises, and Scotland's first 'gay movement club' opened on Friday 11 July 1980. It was christened The Club.

The arrival of an openly gay club in the square did not go unchallenged. Opponents included the Scottish National Institution for the War Blinded at number 2, who objected on general moral grounds, but also complained that their blind clients would be particularly at risk from homosexuals. It makes us laugh now, folk fearing gays would pursue the war blinded, like randy characters in a Benny Hill sketch.

Last night, reading a novel in bed, the square quiet except for the occasional hilarity of students heading home, I came across the following statement 'humour can sometimes be used as a defense against the whip-lash cuts of pain, failure, despair and loss by reducing such things to absurdity'.[3]

Time and distance have rendered comic the image of gays chasing elderly, visually impaired soldiers to sate their lust on. But it is an illustration of how things were. Like Grampian Police, the majority of the population believed that LGBTQ+ people were entirely focused on sex – depraved sex.

Presumably some of the Seaforth Highlanders or war blinded were themselves queer, but to be open about their sexuality would invite prison, violence, rejection and isolation. It was not legal to be gay in the UK armed forces until 2000.

Would I object if a club was to open in number 4 Queens Crescent today? The Club hosted discos on Tuesdays, Fridays and Saturdays. They closed at 1am on

3   C Blackwood, *Great Granny Webster*, New York: NYRB Classics, 2002 [1977]

a Tuesday and stayed open until 2am at the weekend. It was not licensed, but patrons could bring a carryout. Our bedroom is at the front of our apartment. If I had been around back then I would have heard the shenanigans in the central garden. I might have signed a petition for the sake of maintaining the peace. But I am not particularly early to bed, and I like a dance. Perhaps it would depend on what music they played and whether they let me join in.

The Club also hosted a programme of talks, film screenings and student nights.

Lesbians were invited midweek for The Women's Room and Dyke's Delight on a Wednesday Night. My partner Zoë wrote a short story about Dyke's Delight around a decade ago, amused by the combined offering of vegan food and a screening of *The Killing of Sister George*, a hot date.

There is no plaque at number 4 to commemorate its place in the history of LGBTQ+ rights, but until about a year ago there was a handwritten notice in the window stating that its owner would sell the premises for cash. I wish that I had jotted down the mobile number and requested a tour.

The first person to occupy number 4 was James Playfair, merchant, who lived there from 1841 to 1866. A series of private owners follow until 1895 when Mrs Strong is listed as the owner of a private hospital. The premises continued to be a medical establishment for the next three or four decades. In 1911 it is recorded as Sir George Beaton's Nursing Home.

The idea of private hospitals in domestic premises feels odd today, but it was not unusual pre- and even post-NHS. A home for what were termed 'Deserted Mothers' existed at 2 Queens Terrace for decades from about 1927, and there was another mothers' home at 121 West Princes Street from 1934. Small ads in local newspapers as late as the 1960s and 1970s show a clustering of mother and baby homes around our district, places where women could pass their confinement before the birth of their child. There are adverts too for adoptions, suggesting that some of these mothers were unmarried, in a time where it was considered socially unacceptable to be a single mother.

Twice I have met men in their sixties, or maybe their seventies, standing outside our building with a scrap of paper in their hand, looking disorientated. When I asked if I could help, they told me, 'I am looking for the house where I was born.'

Over time some streets have been renamed, buildings renumbered. Some have burnt down; whole blocks have been demolished. It is difficult to work out where houses were or are. I wondered if these men had been adopted from mother and baby homes located in private houses: places of confinement they had no memory of and could no longer find.

The connection of Queens Crescent and its environs to marginalisation and social transgression is in part due to the buildings' dodgy foundations which brought down property prices. It is part of what enabled the Scottish Homosexual Rights Group to make their home at number 4. It is part of the reason Zoë and I could move here too, part of what keeps the place ungentrified, the rogue landlords in business.

We are not living beneath a volcano, but I sometimes wonder if we are living above a sinkhole, if we might suddenly descend into the earth, the way Cardinal Keith O'Brien predicted we would. What an irony that would be.

'It's not what they were, dear, as much as what they were doing in the central garden.'

The Scottish Homosexual Rights Group campaign for decriminalisation was successful in 1980. The victory was a death knell for The Club. Commercial venues, freed from the threat of prosecution, started to compete for the pink pound. The Club remained unlicensed for alcohol and could not compete with the likes of Bennet's, which opened in 1981.

The Club closed in 1982, to the relief of residents of the square who would no longer be woken by the sound of patrons making their way home or revelling in the pleasure garden.

Looking out of my sitting room window, towards number 4, I realise that noise was not the only reason it was not an ideal location for a gay club. The shadows around the central garden offer concealment, but the men who crossed the square to reach number 4 were exposed to a combination of seclusion and prying eyes. It was risky, passing beneath the streetlights to reach The Club. You could be observed.

'It's not what they were, dear, as much as what they were doing in the central garden.'

It is three thirty on Sunday 19 January. I have been writing this piece, on and off for nine days. Yesterday my partner Zoë returned after ten days of working overseas, thousands of miles away from home. Our WhatsApps are full of messages welcoming her back. In a while, I will pop upstairs to feed our neighbours' cat, later we will have dinner together and tomorrow we will both go to work, like regular nine to fivers.

There are four flats in the converted townhouse where we live. Zoë and I are the longest residents. I am now the oldest person in the building.

1980, the year homosexuality was decriminalised in Scotland, was also the year before the first cases of HIV positive people were identified in the UK. I remember the Tombstone Adverts, the sanctioned hatred towards LGBTQ+ people that followed in their wake.

1988 saw the establishment of Section 28, which blighted the lives of LGBTQ+ people, and later still there was the Keep the Clause Campaign, an opportunity for more bile. That campaign was defeated in 2000 when Section 28 was repealed.

Equal marriage was legalised in England and Wales in 2013 and in Scotland in 2014. I have never considered myself the marrying kind, but Zoë and I got Civil Partnered in 2020 after 20 years together.

The Club existed for just over a year at 4 Queens Crescent, a brief moment in the fight for equality in Scotland. The conditions that brought it into existence were centuries in the making, a combination of geology, licensing laws, prejudice, marginalisation and activism. The building itself is still standing, for now. Its ownership unlisted on the land register.

Thirty minutes ago, I left my desk, put on a jacket, scarf and boots. Zoë and I walked across the square to look at number 4 and I remember how in 2018 a collective of Glasgow tenants occupied the building, protesting against the landlord, who happened to be the same person who had been jailed after the fatal fire in Melrose Street and later fined for demanding rent with menaces, despite being barred from leasing any properties. I remembered how the police had evicted the activists, with the rogue landlord in attendance.

Zoë and I walked down Queens Crescent Lane South, a narrow, graffitied vennel by the side of the Great Western Road slip, and looked at the back of the building. We were level with number 4's basement and so it looked taller, more imposing from that side. A rusting fire escape zigzags up to the fourth floor. There is a shiny, new padlock on the gate to the rear of the house, a dead-eyed security camera droops from the roof. We were alone in the lane, but that meant nothing. In the city you never know who is watching you.

It is growing dark. I am back at my desk. The lights are on in our sitting room. I wonder if people crossing the square occasionally look up at our windows and wonder who lives there.

We do.

We live here.

Dedicated to our neighbour Mrs Margaret Smith, who did so much for our community and who taught me a lot about the local history of St George's Cross.

20-Something
Spittal Street

INK ASHER HEMP

When I was in playgroup
They'd roll out a strip of paper the length of the room
And we'd walk through trays of paint at one end
Making our way to the other side
Peeling painted toes from budget parchment
Leaving a trail of prints behind us

If you dipped the shoes of every trans person in Edinburgh
in gloss and acrylic
And then connected together the prints we left – like dot
to dot
You could make a 'community fingerprint'
Of who we are by where we go

One of the lines near its centre would be Spittal Street

Hold out your hand
Palm up
And pick a finger

Geographically, if Edinburgh Castle is the raised bit in
the middle of your fingertip
Spittal Street is one of the lines a couple of mil downhill
to the west
Downhill on the left of your finger
Close to the castle
It's on the route of the open-top tour buses
But there's no stop here
Despite it sharing the characteristics of other destinations
Being well presented and elderly

20-something Spittal Street has immaculate posture
Polite, self assured – but on the reserved side
Not overly forthcoming
20-something Spittal Street is strong and broad
Robust
In good condition on the outside

And inside there have always been Edens

Among a collage of masonry, medical supplies and
box files
Doors with brass handles that are patched with ply
Some closed, decorated with laminated notices and
sellotaped signs
Others open, allowing mismatched filing cabinets to peer
outside
Short ones leaning on tall ones angled by uneven floors
All illuminated by strip lights
Bars of incandescent yellow interspersed with blue travel
though architecture old and new
They line the ceilings of consulting rooms
Starkly sharing miniature sinks, biohazard bins and privacy
curtains

They flicker over the constellation of chairs bolted to the floor of the windowless waiting room

And it's here that an Eden sits
Lanky limbs claiming a chair and a half
Neck reaching to read the posters on the walls
Some peeling, letting you into the secrets of a paint that is a slightly different greenish-blue
To the blueish-green of the rest of the wall that has seen more life

They hold a pen in their left hand and a registration form in their right
They've answered all the questions they can
But some of the multiple choice ones don't fit or don't make sense
So they've scrawled their answers round the edge – in the margins
It's okay – it's 2018
People are still learning
Trans stuff

The receptionist said she'd come and collect their form but there's no sign of her yet
They absentmindedly kick at their bag on the floor to mark the passing of time
Taking responsibility for measuring the stillness of waiting with movement
The clock on the wall appears to have run out of battery

The timepiece in St Cuthbert's Church on Spittal Street stopped moving in 1911
When there was no one left to wind the mechanism

For while the hands revolved beliefs continued to evolve
Merging ever closer
Until two local congregations took the decision to combine
Leaving St Cuthbert's Church empty

One year later its vacant walls became the TB dispensary
As the building was claimed for the worship of the
stethoscope
Pews removed to make way for the installation of internal
skeletal walls
It took an anatomical recalibration to transition to the
altar of the nurses' workstation
But outside society was also reorganising and this
Along with the development of medication
Rendered tuberculosis less and less relevant to Edinburgh
Until one day, when the clock in the doctors' office was
no longer needed to indicate the next appointment
It stopped moving

Now between the hours of 8.45am and 7pm you can turn
up and register as a patient
Inside 20-something Spittal Street you'll find a GP
practice, clinics, drop-ins and dental services
For anyone experiencing homelessness or in need of a
needle exchange
Once you've completed a patient registration form you'll
be offered an assessment with the practice nurse
At 9.15am on Tuesday morning

An Eden, who is 134cm tall
(If you include their woolly hat and boots)
Stands, back against a tape measure
Feeling very short beside the tall nurse who wears a

cardigan that would drown them

The cardigan nurse takes
Their height and weight and blood pressure
Their case history including details about accommodation,
nutrition and sleep

She's going through the motions
They think
Looking at the floor
An abstract patchwork of lino worn, replaced and spliced
Trying to work out which was the original

The cardigan nurse gives
Practical information about how to navigate services and
gentle reassurance

She seems kind of okay
They think
Still looking at the floor
Half waiting
Expecting her to have already asked why they'd skipped
some of the registration form

The cardigan nurse offers
Questions, about what they need and how this process
has been so far
Invitations without pressure or expectation

They look up
Trying to confirm if she's genuine
Words formulating, pondering
They can't be the only one to have found the form
awkward, outdated, right?

So they decide to try
Accepting her invitation
Tentatively beginning to open it into a conversation

And, in response, the cardigan nurse doesn't pretend
To know things she doesn't know
She understands how to learn and how to get things wrong
She commits to talking with the staff team about the registration form
She commits to talking with the staff team about the registration form as many times as is needed

In this moment the cardigan nurse makes potential future healthcare hiccups okay
As enough okay as possible

When they leave the consultation room
The cardigan nurse walks them to the door
The long corridors are fashioned in a way that is vaguely intestinal and not particularly navigable
And the cardigan nurse volunteers that she still gets lost occasionally
So don't worry if that happens at some point
But she wouldn't let that be part of their first appointment

An Eden, wearing well-worn trainers hotly pursued by loose laces, takes the stairs two at a time
They're heading back to wait at reception – not in a rush, just enjoying the movement
Their morning meeting was cancelled so they've arrived at Spittal Street unexpectedly early
So early that the nurse who normally comes to get them isn't here yet

And they'd thought, by now, they'd be able to find their own way round this building
However, it quickly became clear that was misplaced confidence

They're here for the dentist – a filling (not great)
But it's the last one they need
And although it might not be a big achievement for some
They feel a quiet pride for turning up to every appointment
To take their mind off the imminent drilling they continue to prep for a community workshop
Their next task is to put together the slides on trans healthcare

Slide One: The Process on Paper
You're referred to a Gender Identity Clinic
You have a first appointment
It takes at least two appointments for a hormone prescription – if you'd like one
Longer for a surgery referral – if you'd like one

Slide Two: The Process in Reality
The waiting lists for a first appointment are years long
In the range of 1.5–9 years depending on where you live
This is followed by an extensive wait between appointments
Private clinics exist but they aren't a viable solution for many
They are expensive and also have long waiting lists

Slide Three: Are There Alternatives?
Acquire hormones without a prescription – with varying degrees of legality and safety…
Ask GP to prescribe as a harm reduction measure
Protocol requires GP to prescribe but high chance they will refuse

Find a needle exchange if you wish to proceed with self medicating
They will handle blood tests to keep you (as) safe (as possible)

An Eden, who is tense, overwhelmed and tired
Had all the information they needed for their Spittal Street GP appointment
Prescribing guidelines printed at the library
Annotated to support the doctor to understand how they fit into the harm reduction framework
Yellow lines highlighting the critical risks of not starting hormones to their health and to their safety

They'd tried to draft their case clearly and simply
Because they didn't want to come across as overly prepared
Because they know that prepared is often perceived as fabricated
But they couldn't improvise this
Because the pressure to get it right was the only thing left powering their body and their mind

If you have stable housing then you probably fall into the catchment area of multiple GP surgeries
If you're trans you'll probably do some 'market research'
Establishing which is the least likely to be transphobic before seeking out healthcare
But if you live in Edinburgh with no fixed address
And you're trying to access medical transition
20-something Spittal Street is your one attempt to acquire a bridging prescription

If the GP said no, Eden's only option would be illegally

sourced medication
If you want to be crude I guess you could call this process attempted blackmail
If you want to be truthful I guess you could call this process attempted living

They finished trying to explain
Closed their notebook and gripped it tightly
While they waited for a decision that had already been made

To be fair, she had listened
As a person
But that almost made it worse
Because she didn't listen as a person with a job who could do something

And so they left
With a distortion in their footfall
A stuttering in self moving skin, muscle, and bone inconsistently

People assume that waiting is hard because you're static
Watching the world continue
But really, you can't pause a body
So you're watching yourself continue
Your still body still moving
Your still bones still making blood to nourish (unwanted) hormone production

Waiting is drifting in multiple directions simultaneously
Pulled by the currents of biology, time, desire, and need
Each year of patience degrading your structural integrity
Until one too many decisions is made about you

And it's all you can do to leave the room

They navigate through the waiting area with its constellation of chairs
Muscles clenched as they round the corner into the corridor
Breath held involuntarily as if there's no oxygen between them and the exit
And throughout, they are focused so purely on clinging into their skeleton that they don't notice Eden

Who stands on their left by the wall
Who is older than the doorway they are currently walking through
Who reached and pulled its handle before they were aware they needed to
Who chooses to stay here
Assisting those who need to arrive quickly and those who need to leave swiftly
At 20-something Spittal Street

The sound of the door makes a nurse in the office look up from her computer
As expected, it's wide open
A few seconds later it seems to close on its own
And then the chair beside the door offers the shallow noise of someone sitting down
She refuses to move that chair even though no one living ever rests there
She refocuses and opens the next patient's records
Her second last – she's working a half day today
It's only a couple of hours until she can leave at

2pm, an Eden arrives, wondering if it was a mistake not to wear a hat
They're still getting used to the way the breeze chills their scalp
But they haven't wanted to wear one since they finally cut their hair

They descend four steps
And are tidied away off the street into the sniket-y, ginnel-y, alley-ish pathway
Tucked down the right side of St Cuthbert's torso
To queue for an appointment time

They run their fingers along the top of the wall to their right
Dry moss crumbles off
They pinch the spores
Rub them back and forth between their finger and thumb
Exaggeratedly seasoning the floor

Pinching, crumbling, scattering
Crumbling, scattering, pinching
Until the queue moves forward

And an Eden, hair tied back, hanging just below their shoulders for the first time in 68 years
(They are patiently growing it out)
Lifts their hand off the snowy wall to their right
Fingers red and numb from writing their name a couple of times
Takes a breath and heads inside

They choose a seat from a constellation of chairs

Bolted to the floor of the windowless waiting room
Walls adorned with posters
Some peeling, letting you into the secrets of a paint that
is a slightly different greenish-blue
To the blueish-green of the rest of the wall that has seen
more life
And sit down

They're wrapped up in thick heavy clothing
And in their pocket they hold a leaflet from a healthcare
workshop at Trans Pride
Where an Eden who is younger in days and older in life
met this Eden who is older in days and younger in life
And after the session they offered them a photocopied
flyer for 20-something Spittal Street
It is simple, unofficial, typed in arial font
A wee description, little map, phone number, and opening
times
It took Eden who is older in days and younger in life less
than the 30 minutes of the bus ride home to memorise
But still they get it out now and read it
Trace its creases and read it
Turn it over and read it

Until the chill thaws off and they unzip their coat
Unwind their scarf and flex their fingers
Finding sensation
And growing awareness of the previously imperceptible
moments of skin and skeleton
That lived unnoticed when everything was numb
Held at a distance

From the day, years ago, when they withdrew from the
edges of themself

Stopped opening their doors and locked their windows
To close out the weather systems generated by our atmos-
pheric pressure and (political) climate over time

It's only when you start to live in your walls again
Filling yourself from boundary to boundary
That you are forced to acknowledge the moments of space
Where, over time, atoms were taken in error by erosion

And for Eden, acknowledging their accumulated absence
invited the arrival of a grief that still lives in their chest

But they're here for baseline blood work
The second thing they brought in their pocket is their
first box of medication for self-medding

A multi-year waiting list feels irreconcilable to younger
people
Those whose current forever is only three or four times
that long
A multi-year waiting list feels irreconcilable to older people
Who've lived more years than they have to come

So they've decided that these will be their last hours of
waiting
And they're poised for the time when moss and lichen
Will soon grow and grasp
And cling and hold
To remember
The shapes their stone skeleton used to know
Breathe the memory
Of the shapes their body used to hold
Before they were edited by circumstance

This is a process of un-editing and re-editing
Through the imagination of hormones and the chemistry
of biology

Until outside is Eden

Euphoric
Finding joy in the touch of the world, the wind, on their
bare feet
Kicking frantic
Enthusiastic
Soles tinged with tones of greenish-blue and blueish-green

They lie back
Looking up at these sandstone walls so tall and the arched
windows their sills cradle
As they're pushed home in their buggy from playgroup
in clothes now decorated
From stamping and tramping their beautiful three-year-old
feet
Through the trays of colour and onto the paper
Leaving a trail of footprints behind them

I wonder where it will lead from and to as they grow
The dot to dot they'll draw of who they are by where they
go

There will always be transgender children
It's transgender teenagers, adults and elders that are less
certain

Do you get to keep growing when your bones start questioning and it's transness that's answering?
When the world starts to witness you ... when your transness becomes tangible ...
Do you get to keep growing, do you get to keep ageing?

There will always be transgender children
And yes, I wish I could guarantee them healthcare
So that it's there for them – if it's something that makes sense for them
And if it makes sense for them, then it's there at the time they need it, not several years later

But more than that, I wish I could guarantee them healthcare
So that I could guarantee them grandparents – elders
So that I could guarantee them that every Eden will be there
For the living of memories – not just within the remembering

Little Gless Box

JOHNNY McKNIGHT

Whit is a queer space? Is there such a hing?

When I first came oot I hud an idea where I *thought* it wis, where I thought I'd fun it.

Oan the danceflair. That's whit Madonna hud promised me. She said I'd get oan that flair and get intae the groove; tellt me tae vogue; that oan that light up flair I could be like a virgin or a prayer.

How many ae us fun a sanctuary and freedom that first time oan the danceflair, suroonded by ithers like us?

Those lights flashing, the speakers pulsating wi a bassline that ran shivers up and doon oor spines. Dancing in rooms filled wi men wi hellish highlights; a throng ae sweaty mesh vests and damp skinny-fit jeans; glistening airms scratching and clawing at the air, euphoric at how high oor airms could reach. A place where ye could kiss a fella and no huv the fear ae being attacked. Where ye could recreate the routine tae 'Can't Get You Out of My Head' and naebody wid take the piss oot ye. Ma space, ma Queer space, ma Safe space. A flag planted ootside it's door by gay crusaders who took thir first steps oan this brave new wurld like it wis the moon landing. Rainbow flags telling us – this is where ye belong. This is yer space. It's aw fur ye.

But ower time ye start tae realise it's no. It's no really *jist* fur us. That shirtless guy yer trying tae fire intae, turns oot he's straight as a Roman road and is only there fur the two quid pints. The group ae party loving lesbians in the corner ur actually blue-lipped alco-popped hen do's, who hink telling me 'being gay is a waste' is a compliment.

So the airms oan those danceflairs dinnae wave wi quite the same gay abandon. They dinnae reach they heights. The space disnae feel quite so queer. And so, disnae feel quite so safe.

Truth is …

Queer spaces ur rare. They float awa in the wind as easy as the flags ootside them.

So where wis ma first space? The first patch ae land that felt mine. That felt queer. Where I felt free, where I could lift ma airms and be masel … where did I plant ma first rainbow flag?

And I realise, like Dorothy, only withoot the gingham and court shoe, it wis in me all along.

It wis in Ardrossan.

Ma hame toon.

If ye ken the toon ae Ardrossan, ye ken this. We're aw aboot the train stations.

We dinnae huv jist the wan train station. Naw. We're special. Exceptional. We've goat three: Ardrossan South Beach, Ardrossan Town and Ardrossan Harbour.

Yer probably hinking three train stations means this place is sum sort ae megatropolis, wi an Asda, a Morrisons, a Zara and a Jo Malone. Overrun wi overpriced toy shoaps and artisan bakeries that charge a fiver fur a loaf. A toon so large it wid take nearly a guid few days tae walk aroon it. A toon that's really a city in disguise.

Ye wid be wrong.

Ye could walk fae the tap end ae Ardrossan tae the bottom end in aboot an hour. Me wi ma clichéd go-like-the-clappers-gay-walk can dae it in 40 meenits easy. And as fur aw they shoaps? Back then – 1992 – there wis pretty much only a Co-op, a video shoap, two bookies, a cafe, two hairdressers and four chippies. That wis the full entirety ae that stoap oan the line cawed Ardrossan Toon.

Ardrossan Harbour? Well, it hud its day ae glory but in 1992 it sits like Norma Desmond, everyhing hud said goodbye. Forgotten, faded, shipbuilding a long and distant memory. This wis a toon oan its arse. A toon wi a lost identity. A toon trying tae find itsel. A toon a lot like me.

I'm fifteen.

Fifteen and wi enough plooks oan ma face tae pass as a dot-tae-dot colouring book.

Fifteen, and ma voice hus dropped, no by an octave like maist boys, but by wan note. I've a voice so high when I answer the hoose phone people caw me Sadie, talking tae me hinking I'm ma maw.

I wis aeways the boy picked oan at school fur sounding gay. Boys and lassies loved tae take a pop. Lassies in scrunchies – like Mhairi Bastarding Haldcroft – sniggering, pointing and chanting poof, pansy, shirt-lifter.

So I hid. I made masel small. I avoided meeting thir een at school. When ither boys wur oot kicking baws I stayed in the hoose. Alone but never alone.

Cos I hud ma music.

I hud built up quite ae collection ae vinyls.

Tiffany, 'I Think We're Alone Now'.

Sinitta, 'I Don't Believe in Miracles'.

Debbie Gibson, 'Electric Youth'.

7 inches that wid make me close the bedroom door, and practise how I might push ma airms up tae that ceiling when I wis aulder, pushing towards a light I hud nae idea how brightly it could, wid, shine.

3 and a hawf meenits dancing like an electrified eel ahin the closed door ae ma bedroom. God, how many ae us danced in oor bedrooms wi wild abandon, only tae go

tae school discos and pretend oor only moves wur a side-ways shuffle? 3 and hawf meenits ae freedom afore we'd pit the needle back and start aw ower again. That shut bedroom door, where naebody could see me, that wis the only way I could feel free.

And then I goat a joab.

Arran View Amusement Arcade.

A summer joab doon at the South Beach (right next tae that third train station). The arcade wis built sumtime in the mid tae late 70s. Big kinna warehoose looking hing, nae character. A big grey slab wi tiny windaes and roller shutters.

The arcade closed in the autumn and winter. But during the summer this wis a tourist destination at its peak – busloads ae tourists pouring oot fae Glesga, aw coming 'doon the watter'.

Hunners ae folk descending intae this fun-haven that hud everyhing ye could wish fur. Puggies. A cafe. Slush Puppies. A booncy castle. Sand. Mister Whippy ice-creams. The sea. A wee train oan a track that hud the audacity tae caw itsel a roller coaster. Strains ae songs fae yesterday playing doon the promenade – 'My Girl', 'Papa Was a Rolling Stone', 'Saturday Night at the Movies' (which made nae sense cos it wis a Tuesday morning and we wur at the beach).

Ma first joab.

I pretended tae ma bosses I wis 16. Pretended I hud worked places afore. Pretended I wis used tae being in charge. Kidded oan I hud common sense. I hud none. When I ran oot ae vegetable oil fur the chips tae fry in? I added water tae the fryer. Imagine ma horror when it started tae spit and spurt at me; biling hoat oil and water bubbling ower oantae the flair.

I cleaned oot ice cream machines cursing the dober

who'd washed it last season, bits ae minging ice-cream stuck oan the cogs, huving tae use ma nails tae shift them only tae realise it wisnae mouldy ice cream, it wis thoosands ae maggots.

Mopping whit felt like 2,000 square feet ae arcade flair every morning afore the punters wid arrive. Back sweating, back breaking. Blue plastered fingers cos I wis shit wi the serrated breid knife buttering the rolls. Imitating Daniel-san fae *The Karate Kid* polishing aw the puggies, waxing oan, waxing aff, airmed wi a bottle ae Pledge. I stood ootside in the pishing rain, bum bag aroon ma waist filled wi fifty pences, politely telling weans tae take thir shoes aff afore jumping oan the boancy castle tae the soundtrack ae Marvin Gaye singing 'Mercy, Mercy Me'.

I never asked fur mercy in that joab. I loved it. I hud purpose. I wis minted – 10 hours work fur the grand sum ae 15 quid. I could buy an album wi that. I felt like an oligarch afore I'd even heard the word oligarch. I felt safe. Who widnae? Ma bosses wur big burly men who ran nightclubs. Bosses wi dark tans and kind eyes; who hud the ability tae talk wi a fag hinging oot wan side ae thir mooth. Bosses wi speedboats they'd take oot ontae the sea in thir tight fitting wetsuits. Bosses wi necks as thick as the hair oan thir chest. Big, handsome, rugged, nicotine-stained fingered bulging bosses that folk widnae mess wi, which meant – by proxy – they widnae mess wi me.

And I worked hard fur them. Fur that £1.50 an hour I brushed and I mopped and I buttered and I whipped and I slushed and I fried and I waxed oan and aff and I smiled … even tae customers who'd say tae snottery nosed weans, 'give yer money tae the nice lady'. I worked til every vertebra ae ma back ached, til every punter oan that beach front hud Mr Whippy ice cream dripping doon thir hauns in the summer heat, til aw ae ma fingers wur covered in blue plasters.

And ma bosses noticed.

They offered me a new joab.

Whit wis considered the tap joab.

The Change Desk.

So, let me describe tae ye the change desk.

It wis a wee hexagon, plonked in the middle ae the arcade flair. Windaes oan every side. An island amidst a sea ae puggies and shoot 'em ups and horse derbys and air hockey tables. It couldnae huv been mair than wan and hawf meters wide oan every direction. If ye wur claustrophobic ye widnae want tae work in the change desk. If ye wurnae confident ye widnae want tae work in the change desk.

See the folk in that change desk, they sat there like David Hasselhoff fae *Baywatch*. Up in thir tower, watching ower the hale arcade, ready tae pounce oan onybody who wid dare tae tamper wi the machines.

But mair than that, they folk in the change desk wur *seen*. That 360 degree windae boax wis filled wi staff who styled thir hair wi at least two cans ae Elnett hairspray and a tub ae extra-hold gel. They wore lippy. They wore thir guid Benetton jumpers. The folk who worked in the change desk *wanted* tae be seen.

I didnae want that.

I didnae want tae be gawked at in that wee fishbowl.

I said tae the bosses: I dinnae want tae dae it. Imagine me, sitting in there, een ae aw the gamblers staring ye doon. And whit aboot the folk I'd catch banging the machines? The protocol wis ye hud tae get oan the mic and shout at them in a 200 decibel scream 'HAWL QUIT KICKING THE MACHINE OR YER BARRED BAWCHOPS'. This wee high-pitched teenage plook in a boax screaming o'er a loudspeaker? Nae chance.

But they speed-boated wavy-haired bosses wi the full lips and dark tans, they widnae listen tae ma protests, they shot them doon wi wan simple phrase:

'Dinnae be a fanny, get in there.'

So I dae.

Inside that wee gless boax, reeking ae stale sweat, fags and the rusty smell ye get fae auld two penny pieces. Money everywhere, hidden in loads ae wee compartments. Notes upon notes bound in elastic bands; bags and bags ae counted coins; stacked columns ae 50 pences, 20 pences, 10 pences, two pences.

A double snib protecting ye fae the ootside wurld. Nae way fur onywan tae get in.

'Get in, ya wee fud.'

There's a chair in that change desk, wi jist enough room tae rotate it 360 degrees, so ye can keep an eye oan everyhing gawn oan aroon ye.

I see a wee rocket in a Naf Naf cap and Joe Bloggs shellsuit booting six shades ae shit oot ae a two penny pusher. I nervously go tae the microphone, tae shout at him. But I cannae. The words willnae come oot. Years ae trying tae no speak, tae keep ma trap shut, cannae bring me tae use that microphone.

So I bang the windae. I bang it so loud it catches his attention. I make a series ae whit I wid caw butch gestures that say – quit it or yer oot. And tae ma wonder … he stoaps kicking. Raises baith hauns in the air as if that bang oan the windae wis me revealing a gun, he backs aff, steps awa fae the machine, and then, sumhing I've never hud onywan dae up tae this point – he mooths a word tae me – a word I've never heard fae folk ma ain age in basebaw caps: *sorry*.

That's when I realise, this chair I'm sitting oan. It's no jist a chair, it's a throne. A place fur the anointed tae sit and survey thir land. A place that grants whoevers peachy wee arse is pressed upon it power. A place where yer showed … Respect.

The change desk. Ma change desk. Ma little gless boax. Ma little safe boax.

'Oh,' says the boss, 'and ye can play whitever ye like in there. Jist … make sure it's guid stuff.'

He points at sumhing, lower doon, unnerneath the towers ae coppers. It's a cassette tape deck. Unnerneath that, various tapes I wis familiar wi – The Temptations, Four Tops, Abba, Marvin Gaye, … A tape player that controlled the music fur the hale place. Fae ootside the booncy castle tae the sweety shoap tae the cafe tae the arcade flair. It even piped the tunes ontae the shore prom-enade.

'Play whitever ye like.'

I wis soundtracking ma ain day at work … watching punters walk in rhythm tae 'Sexual Healing' while the sun beat doon oan them; weans booncing oan inflatable castles tae the wails ae Martha and the Vandellas.

Efter two weeks ae working in that wee boax I started tae feel sumhing … sumhing changing in me. I wis starting tae feel like this music I wis playing, it wisnae guid enough, it wisnae … me. No this new jacked up, king oan his throne version ae me onyways …

Mibbe it wis the snib oan the door knowing naebody could get in, mibbe it wis the emergency bell I could ring if onybody gave me jip or tried tae get ony money, mibbe it wis the knowledge that a bang oan the windae and a wave ae the finger wid be enough tae pit the shiters up the wee radges … or mibbe, jist mibbes, I wis starting tae get a bit mair at ease wi people seeing me.

And the tunes fae in here? That wisnae ma music. It wisnae ma soundtrack. So mibbe, mibbe it wis time fur me tae make ma ain.

I went hame that night, and started tae dig oot ma vinyls. Hauns sweating, a C-90 blank cassette tape ready tae be recorded oan. It wis time fur me tae no only be seen but tae be heard, ma music playing in ma little gless boax. Nae mair soul singers. Nae mair Motown. Nae songs fae decades that werenae mine.

How many ae us made mix tapes that we wid never dare share wi the wurld?

Well this widnae be wan ae those. Naw. This wis gawn tae be the best, happiest, maist joyful mix tape the South Beach Arran View Amusements hud ever heard.

I arrive fur work the next day, cassette tape in poaket. I clean those puggies, I mop that flair, I open they shutters ready fur the onslaught ae gamblers and shoot-em-uppers. I can hear the wee Maxwell cassette tape shoogle as I move, like sum sort ae percussive reminder.

But I dinnae play that tape. No yet. I sip ma can ae Red Cola in ma gless boax, and I dish oot coppers and fivers worth ae 10ps tae the punters. I watch weans fight wi each ither ower who's first oan the booncy castle. Whit started aff as a cloudly, dreich day hus noo seen the sun break oot fur freedom. Bright, glorious sunshine beating through.

Ma boss fur the day, we'll caw him Tommy, he's no whit ye wid caw a grafter. Whit he is though is a Top Tier Tanner. First hint ae sun and it's taps-aff, jeans replaced wi shorts that wid make Tom Daley question if they're too wee, and he's goat a recliner placed oan the promenade. Right unnerneath wan ae the speakers.

He's like sum sort ae Greek god lying there. Sun catching oan his dark chest hair. Sweat trickling doon his muscular calves. It's here I first looked at a man and felt sumhing ... a deep, submerged sumhin.

Sumhing that wid take anither nine years tae fully translate … taking every bit ae him in, lying there in the sun, me in the safety ae ma little gless boax. I'm allowed tae look in here. It's ma joab.

And the arcade's getting busier noo. Thumps oan the windaes and butch shakings ae ma fist as a warning every few meenits. And Greek God's still baking, I swear I'm seeing his skin go a deeper shade ae broon afore ma very een.

And The Four Tops ur playing 'Reach Out I'll Be There' and I ken it's getting tae the end ae that tape. I ken that it's time … time fur me tae pit ma soundtrack oan. Tae let aw these hunners ae holiday makers hear ma music taste. Tae let ma boss hear ma music. And I feel scared. Like um aboot tae flash ma arse tae the public ur sumhin. Cos at school when people'd ask whit I liked tae listen tae I'd say Wet Wet Wet. I'd say Bros. I'd say Bryan Bloody Adams cos I wisnae fur gien people mair reasons tae take a pop at me. But I'm no at school. I'm at ma work in a joab I'm bloody guid at. I'm in ma wee protected gless boax. I'm oan ma throne. And I dinnae want tae gawk at that big ride ae a boss soundtracked tae an era that isnae mine. So ma blue plastered fingers fumble at the cassette, popping it in, side A. Random punters at machines no even realising the music's aff, the boss cooking in the sun, Mhairi Bastarding Haldcroft fae the year above me at the two penny pushers.

Mhairi.

Bastarding.

Haldcroft.

Her wi the scrunchie and scrunched up nose. Her wi the loudest cackle oot the three witches who'd caw me poofy Johnny oan ma way tae school. Mhairi Bastarding Haldcroft …

Ma haun hesitates tae press play.

I dinnae want her hearing ma soundtrack, ma music, seeing me.

But this is ma space. Not hers. Ma summer joab. Ma arcade. Every day I mop every inch ae this flair. Those puggies? It's me who polishes them. Those bins? I'm the wan who wis meant tae empty them but forgot.

Mhairi Bastarding Haldcroft wi the cruel mooth and vertical fringe? Her flag's no planted here.

I'm oan ma throne, I'm in ma gless boax.

And so I press play.

A long 30 second hiss until the voice ae Janet Jackson rings oot … 'Control'.

The boss looks tae the speaker, aware this is an alien sound and no a Motown classic. Sum auld fella at the derby race track swats the air like it could stoap Miss Jackson fae singing. Mhairi Bastarding Haldcroft halts fae pitting mair money in the machine, it looks like she's sniffing the air, like she can smell the camp. It disnae stoap Janet though. She's speaking in yon American voice wi authority, telling us she's in control. She'll say whit she wants, dae whit she wants, and she's done wi folk telling her otherwise.

The Jimmy Jam and Terry Lewis dance beats kick in. I watch ma well-played movie wi its gallusly refreshed soundtrack fae aw 360 degrees. A gaggle ae lassies over by the Simpsons puggie, two ae them singing alang. The auld derby guy taps his fit. But I can feel wan stare trying tae break gless. Mhairi Bastarding Haldcroft.

Mhairi's looking ower, nose predictably scrunched up.

If we wur at school I'd look awa, or look at the grun, but no here. Not while I'm in ma gless boax. Ma safe space. Naw, I dae the unhinkable. I turn the music UP.

Mhairi Bastarding Haldcroft, in retaliation at ma defiance, boots the puggy. And I dae whit I'd never huv the power tae dae at school but I dae here. I dinnae look awa. I bang the windae, ready fur ma well-rehearsed mime show. Only, Mhairi disnae hear me. How could she, the music's too loud.

So I should turn the music doon, bang again, but tae dae that, tae turn that music doon wid feel like she'd won. Wid feel like they'd aw won. This is ma soundtrack, ma music, this hus been a night ae planning the perfect playlist and I made it tae be played loud … fur that big Greek god ae a boss tae no jist see me but hear me … fur them aw tae hear me … so I reach over … finger trembling oan the tannoy button … hesitating as ma tape noo segueways fae Janet tae Kylie.

Ma gub moves towards the microphone, a nervous lick ae the lips, a wee cough as though it could clear the terror awa.

And Mhairi's looking ower. She knows I willnae dare dae it. She knows I dinnae huv the nerve tae speak up, tae let ma voice be heard. She boots the machine again, a smile oan those thin-as-a-fiver lips.

Kylie's rallying cries fae 'What Kind of Fool (Heard it All Before)' fill the arcade, and I realise she's no singing tae sum auld lover, she's singing tae me.

Kylie's singing aboot no wantin tae hear ony mair excuses, nae mair hiding, nae mair looking tae the flair, nae mair hiding ahin closed doors, nae mair.

This is ma soundtrack.

This is ma castle.

I'm oan a fucking throne.

A voice rings oot. A voice higher pitched than Kylie's; a voice that speaks wi mair authority than Janet's and it's a voice that scares me. It's a voice I've never heard speak wi such confidence, and it's aw the mair surprising because it's mine:

> 'Mhairi Haldcroft, ye kick that machine wan mair time and yer getting that arse booted oot that front door. Quit it. Noo!'

And she looks ower, open moothed. But she stoaps kicking that machine. She backs aff.

Not cos ae sum butch mime show, but cos ae ma high-pitched holler. Soundtracked tae Kylie, and noo merging intae Madonna's urging tae strike a pose. Mhairi Haldcroft looks ower in fury, in rage, knowing in this gless boax she cannae touch me. She cannae harm me. I'm the powerful wan.

And she points at me, then takes her finger and runs it across her throat.

It's supposed tae scare me, and if we wur onywhur else mibbe it wid, but no here. I've planted a flag above this wee gless boax. A rainbow flag held up by the voices ae Janet Jackson, Kylie, Celine Dion, Dannii, Paula Abdul, Madonna.

Mhairi Bastarding Haldcroft mooths, *yer deid.*

She disnae see the flag waving.

She disnae feel the power ae this music. Ae these divas.

She disnae realise I'm no at school, I'm at ma work. She disnae feel ma power.

And as she runs her finger ower her throat again I dinnae listen tae her. I dinnae let ma fear ae her in, naw. I huv ma soundtrack. I huv Madonna telling me whit tae dae.

So I obey Madonna, I strike a pose.

I strike a pose wi wan middle finger up triumphantly at Mhari Bastarding Haldcroft and tae aw those that came afore and efter, because fae this moment oan I realise that I will aeways huv this. I will aeways huv ma safe space. Ma Queer Space. It will aeways gie me new life. There will aeways be me, ma music and ma little gless boax in an amusement arcade.

I huv ma pride flag wi me, flying in the wind, first planted here. Ardrossan South Beach Arran View Amusements.

Ma flag that tells folk: I will be seen and I will be heard. Even if I dae still sound like ma maw.

Nowhere

ALI SMITH

To be honest? There was nowhere.

Honestly it was a bit like there was no room, no place, for honesty itself. This was problematic if you were a person who found dishonesty the kind of troubling that could make you ill.

I'm talking about a time when I was in my teens and early adulthood, in a very fine town (it was still a town, not yet a city in those days) in the stunningly beautiful highlands of Scotland in the 1970s and early 1980s; not that I truly recognised its beauty, or the town's, though I already profoundly loved them both, till I'd left and come back and seen the place again with fresh eyes.

More specifically? Okay: there was school. There was home. There was church on a Sunday. There was working in Littlewoods restaurant every Saturday, then later on the Book-A-Bed-Ahead accommodation desk in the tourist office in the school holidays, where it came in handy if you spoke a couple of different languages; thinking of the tourist office now makes me realise that though none of this is very long ago, it's now close to unrecognisable: most Sundays back then almost everything in town was closed, everything except Barneys shop on Castle Street, which meant that when tourists stood at the front desk and asked us what they could do here on a Sunday we used to tell them how nice it was to *drive or walk a few miles out of town and turn and look down at the view of the Firth, it's a great view.*

Anyway.

<u>School:</u>

secondary. Mixed comprehensive. When I look back now at photographs of the school I went to I see what an unusually attractive piece of pure art-deco/modernist architecture we were lucky enough to be taught in. Most of all I remember its fresh intake of teachers, young and keen and full of life and energy, who saw us through those years with real expertise and grace.

But I also remember this:

one day only a couple of months into my first year (I'd have been 11 years old) I collected my science jotter from the alphabetical pile at the front of the class and saw that somebody had written three capital letters on it in biro next to my name. LEZ.

What did it mean? I'd no idea. Of course I didn't. I was eleven, and I wasn't just prepubescent, I was a total naif, a total innocent.

I mean I worked it out, what it literally meant.

But I knew that what it really meant was that I was being watched, being policed, if you like, by somebody in my own class at school, one of my peers, and that something had been decided about me by somebody, presumably also by their pals.

So I scribbled over it with felt tip till it wasn't legible even to me and I gave up science for languages as soon as I could.

I think back now half a century later and I wonder exactly which small person, which boy or girl in our science classroom (where shortly they'd be teaching us about sex education using the innards of frogs) in our school in our town in mid-1970s highland Scotland was already worldly enough plus foul and bullying enough to write this message delivered directly to me, next to my name on my jotter.

Well. I'll never know. I'd love to, though. I'd like to see their face again, their young face at the same time as their fifty-years-older face, and congratulate them for knowing something about me that I didn't yet know about myself. I'd also like to ask them what kind of life it was they were living themselves back then to think to do such a thing, and then about what we'll call their marksmanship, why they'd thought it was a good idea to mark me out.

Power? Hilarity? Wank? An act of service?

To whom?

All of 11 years old too, whoever it was, or 12 at the most, and let's face it very unlikely to be reading this piece now. But never say never, whirligig of time etc; if it's you who did this reading me now, hello! Remember me? How's your life been? I hope it's been a very good one. Hope you've been happy and well-met in life and in love. I have. My time's been good, thanks, mainly because I've been lucky enough to live at a luckier time in history, so far anyway, and in a luckier part of the world, than a shedload of folk who lived before you and I did, or who are living in countries in the world keener than here to make their lives impossible. We've both lived, me and you, through a time when things got unbelievably better, for me at least, a time totally unthinkable and unimaginable when we were 11 and you wrote on my jotter that approximation at a word for what you'd decided someone other than you was.

Thank you anyway for the very early education. All my best to you.

That's that.

But let's stay thinking about school for a bit longer, because what else there was at school was drama club.

We put on Arthur Miller's *The Crucible* when I was 13 and we were so good we won a Scottish Community Drama award; I played Betty Parris and had to lie in a bed in a coma for most of Act 1, then wake up screaming like crazy. The coma meant I knew the whole first act off by heart and could prompt everybody else sotto voce when they needed it.

I loved drama club. I think it's one of the things that saved me. Decades later, when I knew I was probably definitely gay, I found out, though I'd had no idea at the time, that other people at drama club, even other people in that particular production of *The Crucible*, were gay too. There was a boy whose name I can't remember, a witty and magnetic person, who always had a crowd of people laughing and capering round him in much delight. And there was Tommy, lovely Tommy, kind always, clever and serious, who went off into life and became a translator, I learned much later he was gay too. I remember him with warmth; I can still hear his voice, always deep with thought, a voice like a quiet steady flame lit the core of him. He played Reverend Hale, and now I marvel at how he knew – astonishing in someone who must have been only 16 then – how to play this character that's so harnessed to dogma, mania and obsession as if the man believed these things were the proof of his sincerity.

So there *was* somewhere after all then, even if it was subcurrent, and even as we learned the script for and performed a play so wise to what happened in history and happens over and over again in reality when a community becomes hysterical enough to try and condemn whichever random group of people it's decided should burn.

Okay. Enough about school for now. Let's go home: because thinking of the name *Tommy* has reminded me of a terrible true story. Here it is. When I was a small child, 3 years old, and we went to stay in the south of England with an aunt and uncle who had a farm, I had a crush on a young man there who drove the tractor. His name was Tommy and I loved him because he always lifted me up and let me drive the tractor with him, even turn the wheel with him. When our holidays were over and we left for home, he gave me a soft toy shaped like a tiger. We called it Tommy the tiger.

I still have Tommy the tiger. He's travelled in the back window of every car I've ever driven.

One day I came home from primary school, this will have been the 1960s still, I think, and my parents, who looked shocked to the core, asked me did I remember Tommy from the farm.

Then they told me that he died.

Why? I asked.

They didn't tell me why.

One day, much later, when I was in my 20s, my mother gave me a couple of small black and white photographs of two men. You should have these, she said.

Why? I said. Who is it, who are they?

That's Tommy from the farm, she said, and that's the man Tommy on the farm was seeing, and then people found out he was seeing this man, and after that Tommy shut himself in a barn and shot himself.

Oh dear God.

I think, too, that *oh dear God* is pretty much what my mother and father must've thought at every inkling they had, as I got older, that their youngest child maybe wasn't as straightforwardly heterosexual a person as her brothers and sisters had so far turned out to be.

It didn't stop me being gay, though, or knowing what was true for me.

It just meant I couldn't, and my parents couldn't – there

was no place for it – share much knowledge of what was happening in my life. I'm sorry about that. I'm particularly sorry that my mother died so young (she was 62 when she died, the age I am now) that she didn't get to see the shift in societal understanding that my father did, the shift that's allowed the generations coming up after theirs and mine to live very differently, so much more freely than us. Even though we believed in our times, like every generation does, that we were the most freed-up generation yet.

Here's another typical moment from that oh so liberal time I grew up in. There I am on the couch next to my sister in my sister's house. Right now I'm in my very early 20s. My sister's a decade older than I am. Her husband's sitting opposite me. Their house is the epitome of current fashion; she and her husband have style and taste and are clever and assured and I aspire to them. For some reason we're all talking about Boy George, who is hugely famous at this point.

I take my heart in my mouth. So, I say. What if somebody you knew, like somebody in your family, was like Boy George?

My sister takes a deep breath.

She says, slowly and carefully,

even if somebody I knew, or somebody in my family, was like Boy George it wouldn't mean I would stop loving them.

Then her husband says,

ah but you have to admit, it's homosexuality that caused the fall of the Roman empire. It's not just a sign of the end of a civilization. It's a root cause of the end of a civilization.

Ah.

That's me sighing, then and now.

But then again. There was also this:

we're all round at my same sister's house for Christmas dinner. I'm about 15. One of my brothers, who is 21, has just caused a silence to fall that's as sheer as the blade of a guillotine – everybody round the table stopped in mid-everything, fairytale-frozen – by saying,

yeah, well, I'd be just as capable of falling in love with somebody of the same sex as I am with somebody of the opposite sex, and so what if I did? It's no big deal.

Intake of breath.

Literal silence for three long seconds.

Then all hell breaks loose, my father shouting *for Christ sake Andrew,* my mother shaking her head, everybody arguing. I am sitting very quietly. I glance at my brother, who's still holding his own against the room. I look at my plate. I know he's playing devil's advocate, trouble-making, being controversial for the sake of it to see what will happen. He likes to do that.

But at the same time it is like someone just reached a hand down to me from the top of a tall wall as if to help pull me up and over it, *here. Come on.*

Glimmer of light.

Okay. That's school and home, then.

That leaves church:

let's face it, the place you'd really expect to be refused or reproved. But *oh dear God,* I was fortunate here.

I so was. I know how lucky. This wasn't in my home town though, where something like what I'm about to tell you was unlikely. No, this happened in my university city, a hundred miles away from home to the east. I was still a practising Catholic in those days; our mother had not only determinedly raised all of us as Catholics, she'd also somehow converted my father to Roman Catholicism a decade after they'd got married, simultaneously persuading him to stop smoking, though she herself smoked till the end of her life.

One Sunday I went to Mass in the University Chaplaincy and the priest, who was a really witty and poetic and philosophical speaker, gave a powerful sermon about the holiness and purity of the body, about the spiritual importance of respecting the body, how we had to protect it and attend to it, and how, if we didn't, we were hurting not just the body but the soul, and not just the soul but the body.

After this sermon I was guilt-wracked for days, no, weeks. I was miserable. I didn't know what to do with myself.

So I got my courage up and went back to the Chaplaincy, knocked on his door and asked him if I could speak to him.

Of course, he said. It's Alison, isn't it. Come in. Sit down. What can I help you with?

I sat down. He made tea, gave me a mug. I stammered it out, I told him I was gay.

Oh good! he said. I'm very happy for you.

I blinked at him.

It's such a wonderful thing, what you've just said, he said. Because when we're not brave enough to be true to ourselves, it means we're not respecting anything about ourselves, so how can we be respecting anyone or anything else? Including God. Hurray! Good for you!

Then he said,

I know this, you see, because I'm gay too.

Then he nodded at me and smiled a big smile.

I came out of that place – that most unexpected of places – and stood in the street dazed, just stood for a bit in the dusk amazed.

I know now how lucky I was, and I am, that this

kindness happened to me. I know how easily it might not have happened. I know how very easily the opposite might have happened.

But it didn't.

There's also a sort of postscript to this story. Fifteen years later, when I'd published a book called *Other Stories and other stories*, and I was giving a reading in an Edinburgh bookshop, a smiling man full of bonhomie and warm energy arrived at the front of the queue of people waiting to get their books signed.

He said, do you remember me?

I'd never forget you, I said.

He'd left the priesthood. He introduced me to his partner. I signed their book with love, and wherever he is now I send him my thank you, most days, for the day I stepped body and soul back into the world and even the grey of the pavement beneath my feet was marvellous.

What I mean by this is the way that nothing but love will make a something of every nothing, will turn every nowhere into

somewhere:

for instance, the moment I'd first ever seen this girl, she was in the year below me at school, I will have just turned 17, I walked past her in the corridor and it was like the corridor itself was strange, it was like light was coming from her and this brightness was lighting me up too – and was it true, or was I making it up, that in that moment she'd also seen me, I mean seen me back?

It was true.

It was transformatory too, like the first time she reached and took my hand, in one of our best nowheres, on the sloping grass of the riverbank in our home town late one Saturday night, no one much else around. It's a beauty of a river, by the way, the river that runs through the place that made me, its water running black and strong and very fast, beautiful when it's low and you can see the stones at its edges, beautiful when it's so high up the banks that you fear for the Cathedral. We sat on the slope in the dark, the old Infirmary and the new theatre behind us, the old red War Memorial with the names of the dead on it way over the water across from us invisible, there were invisible bridges to either side of us, we could hear the far traffic on one of them, there'd be rabbits over there out eating the clover in the grass beneath the castle in the dark, the water before us was a glint of shifting streetlight and she took my hand. It was true, then.

I mean, it wasn't ever easy. We learned how to pretend, not just to everyone else but to ourselves as well, that it was nothing, that we were nothing. We worked out how to hide it. We knew not to offend or attract attention. We knew to protect ourselves. We had to.

The repression did us no good. It did quite a bit of damage over the years we were together.

Fast water under those bridges.

Meanwhile we collected the nowheres, the many night-scapes beyond the town through the front and the back windows of my father's car, which he very kindly, perhaps even silently knowingly, often lent me, then through the windows of the clapped-out old Mini we bought, paying half each for it soon after we'd learned to drive. It was yellow with a black roof; she painted a rainbow on it from bonnet to boot. It had a hole in the floor of the passenger seat footspace through which we could see roadsurface passing under our feet wherever we went.

I can still clearly remember the smell of that car, old leather and petrol, the little green tree air-freshener.

Every random road surface a vivid blur of life.

Everywhere we went. Didn't matter where.

THE STRAND

THE STRAND BAR

SCOTTISH BUILDING

Nation Life

Nation Life

Glasgow's Queer Foundations

JEFF MEEK

'May I refresh your glass?'.

These are probably the first words spoken to me in an LGBTQ+ venue. They were uttered by Sam, a 60-something-year-old former journalist who had spied me in the corner of Austin's Basement Bar nursing a pint and appearing quite forlorn.

Spooked by stories of predatory older men, I at first declined, such fears driven by the acute ageism within the community where anyone over 30 was eyed with some suspicion as if the right to queer sociability ended when one entered their fourth decade. Added to this was the entrenched anxiety that at 18 I had yet to reach the homosexual age of consent of 21.

'Don't worry, I am only interested in what's in your head not your trousers.' Suddenly I didn't feel so lonely.

With hindsight, a miserably wet, slushy and dark mid-January Glasgow evening in 1989 was probably not the best choice for my first excursion onto the 'scene' but my desire to be a part of something motivated me to take my first steps. I had plucked up the courage to buy a copy of *Gay Times* from an RS McColl on Waterloo Street and found Austin's Basement Bar listed among the rather limited Glasgow venues. It was described as having a 'friendly atmosphere' and was 'busy weekends'.[1] Perfect for the novice I thought. The door on Hope Street was unassuming, as was the sign above the door. On entering, you descended a flight of stairs that turned right into a quite small, tiled and partly carpeted bar. I seem to remember elements of mirror tiling and chrome. But the most striking feature that cold, wet Friday night was the absence of any heaving mass of queer men and women. At most, there were five others in the bar. It was early, I thought, just gone 7 o'clock, so maybe the heaving mass would arrive later. It didn't. I ordered a pint of heavy tops and sat in the far corner where there was cushioned corner seating and a good view of the bar, hoping no one would see me. But Sam had broken through the ice of isolation and offered camaraderie and amity.

If you identify as lesbian, gay, bisexual, trans or queer/questioning (LGBTQ+), your formative years as an adult can feel distinctly lonely, isolated and devoid of community. This was especially true for those of us who came of age in Scotland during the 1980s and 1990s. At that time, sex between consenting male adults in private had only recently been decriminalised (through the Criminal Justice (Scotland) Act 1980), the HIV/AIDS crisis had emerged, and the notorious Section 28 of the Local Government Act of 1988 had been introduced. Growing up in such an environment meant that your life was often shaped by anxiety, fear and condemnation, along with a deep sense of marginalisation. Yet the city offered something I and many others always craved: anonymity, and the potential to begin a new life, freed from the confines of our past. As a stranger in the city, no one knew me or my history;

1 'Round Britain Gay Guide', *Gay Times*, November 1989, p93

I had a clean slate, far removed from the small farming community where I grew up. I was 18 when I moved to Glasgow in late 1989, living alone in a city of strangers. Yet this anonymity would eventually lead to a new sense of isolation and loneliness, and the search for community and company would lead to specific places and spaces within the city that would play an important part in my sense of identity and belonging, and in my social and sexual liberation.

Scotland underwent a notable but often overlooked cultural shift during the 1970s. This was a decade where LGBTQ+ activism in Scotland took root and prospered with the continuing labours of the Scottish Minorities Group (SMG, later the Scottish Homosexual Rights Group and Outright Scotland). Their work with politicians, religious leaders, medics and the police paved the way for legal change (and to some extent social change) during the 1980s. It is no surprise then that at the same time as the SMG was advocating for LGBTQ+ civil rights others were developing a commercial scene catering for LGBTQ+ Scots. The building at 183 Hope Street in Glasgow looks like any other Victorian shop and tenement structure in the city centre. There is nothing remarkable about this sandstone structure, replicated in form and function throughout the city. Yet its inherent ordinariness belies its significance in the modern queer history of Glasgow. From the years immediately following the Second World War right until the late 1990s, this building housed venues central to the leisure, commercial, romantic, companionate and sexual opportunities for LGBTQ+ Scots. It certainly was for me.

I accepted that pint and over the next few weeks, I would occasionally bump into Sam, either in Austin's on Hope Street or Squires Bar, West Campbell Street. During these meetings in the two bars which would become central to my life in Glasgow, Sam often reflected on his 40-odd years on the gay scene in Glasgow. He viewed the scene not as some static and immovable cluster of commercial enterprises but as an ever-changing and malleable response to the demands of its clientele. As the clientele changed so did its demands. I was surprised to learn that there had been a 'gay scene' in Glasgow since the end of the Second World War, but it was a different scene then. He mentioned visits to various bars in the 1960s before the emergence of a commercial scene, such as the Royal Restaurant & Bar in West Nile Street, the coffee bar in the Central Station Hotel, and the Top Spot at the Theatre Royal. As we sat one evening in Austin's, Sam explained that he had been coming to this bar since about 1957, when it was The Strand Bar and Restaurant. At that time, it was 'mixed', but Sam laughed as he recalled that 'it was always heaving with queens at the weekend'. Several times, new owners had attempted to 'rebrand' to push out the 'queens', but they kept coming back. 'My friend Agnes was a lesbian and we would always go there together, just so we looked straight.' Sam recalled numerous pleasurable times at the various bars but also highlighted just how risky it was to be gay in Glasgow at that time, with the threats coming from the police, homophobic Glaswegians, but also from some who claimed to be part of that community. Yet the bar, whether under the name of Austin's or The Strand, was a beacon for LGBTQ+ Glaswegians, a place offering community and safety.

The importance of Austin's was not just related to the emergence of a new commercial venue for LGBTQ+ Scots, but also that it was housed in a building with a long history of attracting this clientele. The original building, a large townhouse with a main entrance on West Regent

Street, was erected in the 1800s, before quickly being converted to commercial premises by the 1860s. It was further converted to apartments and shops by the notable Glasgow architects Salmon, Son and Gillespie in 1905.[2] 183 Hope Street, just around the corner from the building's original entrance, hosted several commercial leisure venues throughout the first half of the twentieth century, operating variously as Rupprecht's, the Lansdowne Restaurant and Bar, and the Kelburn Restaurant, with the premises becoming The Strand Bar and Restaurant shortly before the Second World War. Throughout the 1960s and 1970s, The Strand was a notable venue for variety artists, singers and comedians, including Bert Coen, Betty Rogers, The Tommy Maxwell Quartet, Billy Hygate, and many more, but from the 1950s The Strand had also become a very popular meeting point for queer Scots. This was in the years before LGBTQ+ leisure became mainstream, in the years when sex between consenting male adults was a criminal offence, and the wider queer community faced considerable hostility and persistent stigmatising discourses. But, as Sam had noted, the threats also came from within the community.

'There was lots of trade or TBHs [to-be-hads], straight guys, who would go gay for the right person,' Sam claimed, 'But there were also lots of rent boys, some of whom were honest and reliable, but others were trouble. I can recall at least two men who were murdered by young men they thought were "available". One of them I knew in passing. Willie Vincent.' Vincent was apparently a 'chicken-hawk', Sam continued, 'who frequently picked up young men in The Strand. Vincent was also a "snitch" and was involved

2 Historic Environment Scotland Listed Buildings, '79 West Regent Street and 183–191 (Odd Nos) Hope Street', portal.historicenvironment.scot/designation/LB33258, accessed 10 October 2024

with various criminals in the city. I think he was just desperate to be liked, to be noticed. I guess we can all identify with that.' As a relative, and nervous, newcomer to the scene, these were perhaps not the stories I wanted to hear, but as someone who appreciated history and 'good tales', I was intrigued by the darker history of the scene. It was not until years later that I delved a little deeper into the Vincent story. I had wondered whether Sam, being a journalist, had embellished some stories, but right enough, William Vincent, a car dealer and police informant was indeed murdered by a young man he had first met in The Strand. The newspapers, perhaps predictably, painted Vincent as an aged predator, positioning his murderer, Robert Scott, 21, as a victim of Vincent's sexual obsessions.[3] Whatever the truth, Scott – who had been discharged from the army as a result of his 'psychopathic personality' – strangled Vincent and drove to England with the body in the boot of Vincent's car, and soon after being convicted of murder he took his own life.[4] It was odd having this connection with a man who had known Vincent. It was a connection with a different Glasgow and a different bar. The two public houses may have shared some of the same building, but things had changed, I hoped.

Such stories positioned The Strand as a location for queer sociability, but one imbued with risk, both external and internal. Perhaps it is no coincidence that as the commercial scene developed in Glasgow, many new bars were located in the basements of existing buildings. Their purpose was in many ways obscured from the public gaze, either behind conventional facades or through being

3 'Evil Man Turned Boy to Killer', *Daily Record*, 9 July 1958, p9; 'Strange Life of William Vincent', *Daily Record*, 15 April 1958, p1
4 'Lifer Hanged Himself', *Aberdeen Evening Express*, 15 December 1959, p1

concealed beyond sight in the bowels of Victorian office buildings. By the 1980s, The Strand was gone, but in the late spring of 1986, Austin's appeared in the basement of the former Strand as a separate entity with the new address of 183a Hope Street. The bar was the creation of Robert Austin, an entrepreneur and former barman at Vintners (at that time Glasgow's oldest LGBTQ+ commercial venue). Austin's would provide competition for existing LGBTQ+ venues in Glasgow, chiefly Squires on West Campbell Street, Vintners on Clyde Street, the Waterloo Bar on Argyle Street and, close by, the Duke of Wellington (the last three hiding their queerness behind facades of traditional public houses).

In tandem with an emerging LGBTQ+ rights movement in Scotland (spearheaded by the SMG), queer commercial venues began to flourish despite the legal restrictions still in place. *Gay News* had visited Scotland in 1972 and lamented the absence of accessible venues for LGBTQ+ Scots, noting that only the Close Theatre offered scope to meet and socialise, describing the venue as a 'stunning exclamation mark in the heart of the old Gorbals'. Glasgow was unfavourably compared to the capital with the magazine noting that 'Glasgow and Edinburgh have unmistakable identities ... Glasgow is a city of superlatives: best Victorian city in Europe, highest high rise, greatest programme of urban motorways, brilliant parklands ... and yet bad for gays.' The capital is presented as a more welcoming and inclusive city and the article suggests that 'gay people relocating should give serious thought to settling in Edinburgh'.[5] Returning five years later, the magazine highlighted the variety of venues now established in Glasgow. Some had existed for several years, including

5 'Gay Life in Scotland or Och, Yerra Naffie Big Jessie, Jimmah!', *Gay News*, Issue 1, 1972, p5

The Strand, which visitors were encouraged to avoid as 'it's rough and some of the people there are rent', others were new and often fleeting.[6] One man I interviewed for my first book examining gay and bisexual men's experiences in post-war Scotland,[7] 'Stephen' (b1939) told me that The Strand was 'rough, rowdy ... really working class' and explained how the scene in the 1950s and 1960s was very much divided along social class lines. 'I remember a few catfights, posh boys looking for trouble, you really had to watch what you said, and that was just amongst the gays', he recalled.[8] Thus, entry onto the scene was ripe with the possibilities of pleasure, community and succour, but was also occasionally risky. That risk may have been serious, such as the dark clouds of HIV/AIDS during the 1980s and 1990s, and ever-present homophobia, or less serious such as interactions with the 'wrong' person, for example the man my friends and I called 'Bandana man', an Austin's regular, who was very personable at first but very quickly turned disagreeable. But the risk was always present. While we always faced the possibility of homophobic rants or physical violence, entry into a queer venue offered a form of sanctuary. For me, Austin's or Squires, just five minutes apart, offered that sanctuary.

The fact that Austin's was a basement bar with entry off Hope Street and down a flight of internal stairs, made the bar appealing. In effect, descending those stairs took you into a different, safer world. Despite the progress made in terms of LGBTQ+ rights, this was still a period where homophobia was common, and violent assaults of queer people were frequent, thus the 'hidden' nature of

6 'Glasgow', *Gay News*, 24 March–6 April 1977, p15
7 Jeffrey Meek, *Queer Voices in Post-War Scotland: Male Homosexuality, Religion and Society*, Basingstoke: Palgrave Macmillan, 2015
8 'Stephen', interviewed by author, 19 March 2007

many venues was important for safety and anonymity. Indeed, as my confidence within the scene developed, I gathered a small group of friends: Bouncer Graham, Fraser's Kenny, Nurse Colin and David, the last of whom I had known since we were five years old. The curious thing about this friendship group was that few of us knew each other's surnames. Perhaps this was a legacy of the past where anonymity was vital for survival. 'Stephen' had recalled that in The Strand gay men adopted 'camp names', generally the forenames of famous female actresses or singers. This was done so that should an 'intimate' conversation be overheard, it would appear to be related to heterosexual relationships: 'I slept with Sophia last night' rather than 'I slept with Stephen last night'.[9] I never knew, or asked for, Sam's surname, nor he mine. We did not exchange phone numbers or addresses. Our friendship was situated firmly on the 'scene'. But it was no less of a friendship for that.

A night out for us in Glasgow in 1989 through the early 1990s generally involved the 'pink triangle': Austin's, Squires and Club Exchange (Club X). Like Austin's, Squires Bar was 'straight' during the day, serving food to passing shoppers and local office workers. It opened in the spring of 1982 (coinciding with the opening of the famous Bennet's nightclub in Glassford Street) and owners Michael Comrie and Norman Walker explained that 'we thought Glasgow needed a trendy-looking gay place'. Comrie and Walker remodelled the existing Whistle Lounge Bar which had entrances at 106 West Campbell Street and 225a West George Street (oddly the bar was listed with the former rather than the latter address, which seemed the main entrance to the bar). During its first few

9   'Stephen', interviewed by author, 19 March 2007

years of trading, the bar made efforts to attract a 'gay-only' clientele, initially employing a doorman to 'filter out straight people in the evenings',[10] but it took some time to establish itself as an LGBTQ+ venue. By 1989 though, it was one of the most popular bars in Glasgow for LGBTQ+ patrons and for several years it directly competed with Austin's for custom, with *Gay Scotland* noting in 1991: 'In Glasgow, something interesting is happening between Austins and Squires – people don't seem to be sure which one to go to! For a long time, Austins was always the busier of the two ... However, it seems that Squires has become the more popular pub at the moment.'[11] In truth, many patrons simply vacillated between the two venues. We would generally begin the evening in Squires, move down to Austin's (or vice versa) and then head for Club X at 11pm. But a night out always involved both Austin's and Squires.

As the premises for wine and sherry merchants, 106 West Campbell Street had a long association with alcoholic beverages, stretching back to the 1890s. In 1969, The Whistle was opened, and the location became a public bar, which it would remain until 1982, when Squires became the newest addition to Glasgow's developing LGBTQ+ commercial scene. Despite both Austin's and Squires operating as LGBTQ+ commercial venues, they had different vibes. While Austin's was rather trendy for the period, Squires looked and felt like a traditional bar. And while Austin's was regularly home to the incomparable musical act Robert and May Miller, Squires opted for frequent DJ nights. Entertainment was important (perhaps not as central as today), but at the heart of both of these

10 'Seen-On-The-Scene', *Gay Scotland*, May–June 1982, p6
11 'Happenings', *Gay Scotland*, Issue 56, 1991, p31

venues was that they offered support and provided a sense of belonging. And that was an experience shared by countless LGBTQ+ people across the period. When I interviewed several gay and bisexual men over a decade ago, I asked them about the part the 'scene' played in their lives.

Joseph (b1959) reflected on his visits to Squires, noting that it was 'like getting out of prison. People were socialising, people were there to enjoy themselves ... It was a revelation.' Joseph had initially considered his sexuality mentally conflicting and confusing, but he was surprised to discover that 'if people [in the bars] were also fucked up and screwed up it was not obvious'.[12] Duncan (b1941) considered his visits to the scene in Glasgow as affirming and educational. 'I met different people who were musicians, pianists ... bus drivers ... farmers ... it was actually very good for me to experience a whole range of people.'[13] There is a common thread running through such experiences which positions the scene, whether it is Squires, Austin's, Vintners or elsewhere, as providing multiple opportunities: personal, professional and intimate. But more than that, the scene offered in effect a community or family of choice. This was the case for Chris (b1959), who commented that the people he met on the scene 'were family and in actual fact, I know ... I've heard a number of gay men describe it that way, but that's exactly what it was, it was another family'.[14]

One of the strengths of the commercial scene in Glasgow during the late 1980s and 1990s was its relative intimacy. It was a small scene, condensed into a handful of venues. You quite often saw the same faces in different bars. Like Sam. When I think of Sam, I associate him with Austin's

12 'Joseph', interviewed by author, 11 July 2008
13 'Duncan', interviewed by author, 5 October 2007
14 'Chris', interviewed by author, 1 February 2008

and Squires, pints of heavy, and long discussions about LGBTQ+ history and Scottish politics. There was comfort in that familiarity, that intimacy, but all that changed in the late 1990s with an expansion of venues within the Merchant City. Entrepreneurs were finally recognising the potential profitability of the 'pink pound'. A more confident, and younger, LGBTQ+ community demanded choice, and venues which offered diversity in music, style and entertainment. As Sam had noted, the 'scene' was not static, it has constantly responded to commercial demands. Squires was suddenly rather marooned at the far edge of the city centre. Sadly, it was gone by 1998, and eventually the seafood restaurant Gamba took its place. Austin's moved to 61b Miller Street in 1999, drawn by the emerging LGBTQ+ commercial scene in the Merchant City, but this proved short-lived.[15] I remember Sam remarking that the move to the Merchant City was like putting a Queen Anne chair into a room designed by Le Corbusier. I remember nodding along but having little clue of what he meant at the time. The advertisement for the sale of a lease at 183 Hope Street was almost a lament to a lost queer paragon: 'City Centre basement bar decorated and maintained to a very high standard'.[16] Squires was no more, Austin's was no more. In the commercial history of any city, businesses come and go, but the demise of both these bars marked a sombre moment in the lives of many LGBTQ+ people of that generation. Both of these venues were more than purveyors of alcohol; they were the fixed heart of a community.

Without Austin's and Squires, I don't really know how I would have coped. I often walk by 183a Hope Street

15 'Glasgow LGBT History Walk', OurStory Scotland, 2014, p7
16 'Lease for Sale', *The Scotsman*, 13 October 1998, p30

and quietly mourn the passing of Austin's. I think Sam would have too. I last saw Sam in Austin's once it had moved to Miller Street. We spoke briefly, and he expressed his disappointment at the new venue. I never saw him again. These places acted as a social seam, and once that was unpicked, it rather quickly unravelled. But I should not feel too sad; the scene has developed significantly since the 1990s and it is a much bolder, much more open and more colourful environment.

I hope others remember Austin's and Squires as fondly as I do. These pubs were instrumental in the creation and nurturing of the LGBTQ+ community in Glasgow, and their histories inspired me to create LGBTQ+ historical maps of Glasgow and other cities. I still remember Austin's and Squires, and I miss them, just like I miss David, who died in 2021, and Sam, and the others who I have not seen for 20 years. While they may have gone, they have left an impression and continue to do so. Unlike Vintners, whose building is long demolished, or the Duke of Wellington, which apparently contains nothing but support beams for the building which sits upon its plot, the skeletons of Austin's and Squires remain. I have not set foot in those venues which came after. I want to remember them as they were.

Earth Inferno

EVER DUNDAS

As a child, I was a portal seeker.

An escape from a society I found confusing and baffling, aye, but I wasn't simply running away; it was a quest. There were other strange worlds within this one, other queer[1] creatures. I knew it. My body trilled with it. You just had to know where to look, how to listen for it, how to sniff it out.

I wasn't looking for transcendence. I'm an earthy bastard, always have been. I didn't want an out of body experience; I wanted immanence.

But that queerness and confidence was obstructed.

I was bullied in high school, spending every day wired for abuse, tense with expectation. After decades of struggle, I only recently had it confirmed that I'm autistic and so much of my life that was confusing now makes sense. It's a story repeated by many autistic people: my peers and teachers sensed my queerness, knew I was different before I did, and went for the jugular.

That experience doesn't make you stronger; it means you carry hypervigilance into adulthood, permanently

---

1   In this piece, the word 'queer' can mean sexuality, gender, or the problematising of norms that is Queer Theory, or various dictionary definitions along the lines of odd, weird, anomalous, etc. It can also mean all of these at once.

ready for battle, and you struggle to find joy in embodiment. My body was ruled by the past, an assemblage of experience, and I wanted to disassemble and reform, but I was stuck, fixed, desperate for a way out. 1996 began with me, lonely and overwhelmed, about to step through a portal that could have been one-way, that might have arrested all my messy potential.

But the earthy bastard I am, I returned. And there was joy awaiting me in darkness, through a queer portal on Victoria Street, slipsliding into goth club Earth Inferno's heady strawberry-scented smoke machine mist, the incantatory music luring me to sticky-floored, sweaty-bodied abandon, the antagonistic surface-world and my corporeal discomfort falling away.

Defiant glamour

Before this haven, there was my first bar and first taste of adult life post-school: The Blue Moon. It was a queer bar and cafe in Edinburgh's New Town that I frequented with my clique of outsider pals from high school. We'd sit in the cafe upstairs eating nachos amidst daft banter, or we'd descend to the quiet bar below and take control of the jukebox. It was dominated by mainstream pop that didn't interest us, so we'd drive the bar staff mad with a constant rotation of 'Should I Stay or Should I Go' and 'The Love Cats'. Despite loving The Blue Moon's warm embrace, with The Clash on repeat, group tequila shots, boozy coffees, watching my pals play pool, and my first kiss, there was something missing. I wanted more, and I accidentally found it one day when someone took me to an Old Town bar and I encountered dark glamour and music I could dance to in the depths below.

Unlike the Apollonian New Town, with its order and precision, Edinburgh's Old Town is a hilly farrago of layers that can baffle both newcomers and modern tech. It was amidst these confusing layers that the goth club Earth Inferno existed, in a strange hovering interstice between the respectable Victoria Street and the grungy Cowgate, simultaneously above and below ground. It hovered here up until the late 1990s, when the mainstream club Espionage took over. In the mid-1980s the club had originally been The Backroom, showcasing post-punk and goth, a defiant glamour that emerged out of the grim early years of Thatcher. Clubs were important to the evolution of the UK goth scene, with Leeds' Le Phonographique arguably the main catalyst from 1979 onwards, followed by London's The Batcave, and with many of the core goth bands emerging from the north of England.

When Edinburgh's The Backroom came to an end, the club went through various iterations until Earth Inferno was born in 1992. Run by Marion Andrews, and previously called The Mission (or 'The Mish'), the three floors of clubs, in basement levels from the perspective of the Victoria Street entrance at the top of the hill, but ground floor and above at the exit on the Cowgate to the rear of the building, were renamed The Rocking Horse. For the Earth Inferno floor, she approached James and Julia Lile (who currently run goth club Ascension) to host a goth night with their friends and soon-to-be resident DJs, Colin Davie and David Downie. When I spoke to James about that era he said the goth scene in the early 1990s, on the street level, 'just died. The whole scene disappeared', and they only had around 20 to 30 punters, but 'within a year word gets out, that for people who are a wee bit different, it's a safe place to go', and when my friends and I went in 1996, the club was a hoaching mass of joyous goths, punks and other misfits sparking off each other, setting the night alight.

'It felt like family'

Recently I gathered some of the regular Blue Moon and Earth Inferno gang for cocktails, and we discussed what the space meant to us. Kat said she wasn't that into the music, preferring the floors beneath Earth Inferno where she'd often go to dance, but she emphasised that 'the goth floor was the community. I liked the feel of it, the atmosphere, and the people', a camaraderie lacking on the other floors. My friend Kath, who had just come out as gay in 1996, captured the importance of this queer space for us outsiders: 'It was being around other people who were also different. It felt like family. You didn't have to justify yourself or feel weird; it was a connection. Even an unspoken one – even sitting next to somebody and watching people on the dancefloor, you felt like you fitted. I don't think I've ever felt like that at any other nightclub.'

Saturday night became a ritual. We'd gather at a friend's house for pre-club drinks as we listened (primarily) to The Sisters of Mercy (or the poisonous gift that was The Sisterhood album) and transformed ourselves, sharing make-up, clothes, and doing each other's hair, before walking across the Meadows to jeers of 'goth!', 'It isnae Halloween haha' and 'You've got a hole in your tights, love' which, while annoying, was at least better than being beaten up. We'd tumble down the Nicky Tam's stair to land in the club, lured by music and the sweet scent of the smoke machine into the cave-like Earth Inferno, with its low ceiling, white and rough-hewn stone walls (later to be painted with skulls, bats and gravestones) and rows of arches with a tiny and crowded seating area. It felt like a deep cellar, a forbidden, deviant place full of secrets. Squeezed into a dark corner was the DJ booth. To plug in the equipment meant having to brave a crawlspace into an old frozen-in-time kitchen, which James and Julia said still had 'knives with blood on them and meat hooks up on the wall'. Next to the booth was a row of seats stretching to the exit, usually commandeered by our gang. The bar was on the far side of the dancefloor, buzzing with punters stockpiling booze because of the cheap 'before midnight' drinks offer. Beyond the bar were what was ostensibly the women's toilets, which had a large dirty pink reception area with sinks along one wall and huge mirrors along the other, where people of any gender would be preening themselves, sharing make-up and posing for photos.

Refreshingly, there was no gender policing of this space: it was never an issue, and likely would have been hard to enforce given the goth look is, as Professor Patricia MacCormack notes, 'highly gender ambiguous, if not gender irrelevant'.[2] Earth Inferno was a delicious escape from the controlling gender norms of everyday life, a taste of how things could and should be, and I loved the glamour and freedom of it. As author and musician John Robb says of goth, 'Clothes mattered' and 'anything goes ... It was sometimes genderless, sometimes gender-full and sometimes the gender was pumped up to the max and always with the borders as blurred as their mascara ... Gothic sexuality was fluid, borders often as blurred as the genders.'[3] This mixing of genders meant the small space off the dancefloor was a perfect timeout for everyone, and you'd often find people in the little alcoves beneath the mirrors, where you could rest alone, smoking a cigarette, or gather in huddles to chat without having to shout over the music, before rushing back out to the dancefloor when summoned by a favourite song.

The irony is that one of my favourite club anthems,

2 P MacCormack, *Death Activism: Queer Death Studies and the Posthuman*, London: Bloomsbury Academic, 2025
3 J Robb, *The Art of Darkness: The History of Goth*, Louder Than War Books, 2023

The Sisters' 'Body Electric', a damning inversion of the joyful Whitman poem,[4] is a portrait of skeezy drug-fuelled clubbing, with their other club-inspired song, 'Floorshow', not much better. Both contain truths, capturing the scruddy side of the alternative club scene, warning me away from rose-tinted nostalgia, ensuring I don't position Earth Inferno as a queer goth utopia. Humans are messy, and the club had its share of cliques and infighting, intoxicated youths bouncing off each other, making dubious decisions and getting into gnarly situations with the wrong people. But that's part of your teens and early 20s: the chaos, the griminess, the mistakes. Most spaces involving humans include people who try to drag you down; I only wish I'd had the secure foundation to deal with it effectively and not press repeat. But, overall, the club was a positive experience, and my friend Chris recently mentioned how important it was to him: 'Because my parents were so distracted and home was such a scary and uncertain environment, I needed this catharsis, the club was kind of like an exorcism ... I think there's a really strong healing aspect.'[5]

Skinkleglam on the dancefloor
I've lived in the Old Town for over 20 years, but in the 1990s I was on the outskirts of Edinburgh and, like most teens, I was desperate to be in the scrum of the bustling city; my life, work and friends were all there, and I resented the exhausting commute home. Dreading the journey one evening, I made the mistake of asking a conservative

4   The Sisters' singer and lyricist Andrew Eldritch riffs off the Walt Whitman poem 'I Sing the Body Electric', a celebration of embodiment and connection. The Sisters song is the inverse: an astute exploration of alienation set in a nightclub.
5   Thanks to those who gave their valuable time to be interviewed for this piece: Kat Husbands, Kath Gordon, Cinn Curtis, James and Julia Lile, and Chris Read – it was a joy chatting to you all.

Christian relative to pick me up from The Blue Moon to take me home. I was interrogated on why I'd been in a gay bar.

'What is wrong with you? Why are you doing this to me?'

'I'm not doing anything to you; I just went to a bar with friends.'

I was lectured the whole way home and when we arrived they said the music I listened to was evil and I should take my CDs and smash them in the back garden. I laughed, but they weren't joking. Fortunately, they didn't attempt to force it. The sudden shift in focus might seem abrupt, but they'd always considered certain music to be a corrupting force, so *obviously* it was to blame for me being in a gay bar.

Given The Blue Moon incident, I kept Earth Inferno to myself, the reaction of my friend Kath's parents consolidating my choice: 'When I came out and told my parents I was lesbian at 17, they were fine. They used to wear the rainbow ribbon; my mum was very proud. When I bleached my hair and started going to a goth club, they were like, "What is wrong with you?" They thought all my friends were into devil worshipping.' This makes our lives sound way more exciting than the reality. While it's easy to laugh at how absurd it is, the Satanic Panic of the 1980s and 1990s destroyed lives (the USA's West Memphis Three case being one of the most famous examples), and goths faced violence in the streets.

One of the definitions of 'queer' is to 'spoil' or 'ruin', and goths cut an aesthetic swathe through social norms as we spoiled and ruined our way through the streets in a haze of hairspray, ignoring mainstream beauty trends and eschewing gender norms. Describing one night when someone was giving them grief, James said, 'We're working class, so we chirp back,' and it ended with Julia in A&E, the police telling her she got what she deserved because of how she looked. Similar happened to James at a football match, the police making their disgust clear, refusing to do anything because of his goth aesthetic. James and Julia emphasised that the club itself was a safe space: you could dress up and be who you wanted to be without any hassle, and sexuality-wise people 'would feel comfortable. We'd look after each other.' In Chris Brickley's book *Heartlands*,[6] he quotes John Kilbride emphasising this element of goth clubs, saying that in the 1980s, 'with institutionalised homophobia and AIDS hysteria, the goth scene created a space where straight, gay and lesbian and queer could mix without any prejudice. We were, at the end of the day, all outsiders together.' This was also very much my experience of the goth scene in the 1990s, and James and Julia talked about one of their friend's coming out as a gay man after the experience of 'getting to wear make-up on a Saturday night and feel safe. Lots of people from the [queer] community used to come.'

John Robb describes goth clubs as 'safe havens where the freaks could come out to play',[7] which attracted me given how alienated I felt by 1990s UK culture and the banal patriotism of Britpop and other mainstream music (excepting Manic Street Preachers' and Suede's bite, glamour and gender play). For me, Earth Inferno was an apotropaic haven, where I wasn't bullied by peers or let down by adults, a liminal space where I didn't have to conform to social norms.

Because of my school experience, I was stiff, awkward, and eternally hypervigilant, prone to what I thought were

---

6   C Brickley, *Heartlands: The Original Goth Scene in Scotland*, Brickley Books, 2024
7   J Robb, *The Art of Darkness: The History of Goth*, Louder Than War Books, 2023

panic attacks and exhaustion, but were autistic meltdowns and shutdowns, as I struggled in a world not built for me. I don't have charm or the gift of the gab, and my ability to 'mask' (faking allism[8] by performing social norms) has always been ropey at best. There's so much pressure in the everyday world to communicate verbally, and conversation is a minefield of taken-for-granted allistic norms, games, subtexts, traps. I've frequently failed at these games over the decades, but at Earth Inferno I could don my trashy grunge-goth garb and experience a communal connection without having to engage in difficult small talk or attempt to make sense of unwritten social rules that regularly left me baffled. Communication was via a shared cigarette or drink, the excitement when a favourite song threw you all onto the dancefloor, the grinning joy as you connected with the stranger in front of you through the mutual love of music. There's the mainstream cliché that goths are miserable bastards but that wasn't my experience; we'd forged a space for ourselves and it was exuberant. John Robb highlights that 'the music was intense, powerful, and sometimes melancholic, but never dour. Most importantly, you could move to it.'[9] In Earth Inferno, I let outside pressures go: I was skinkleglam on the dancefloor, embodied present tense, pure immanence as music exorcised my rage, slipping me into sensual efflorescence.

Sulphurous centre of the world
The Rocking Horse comprised three floors of music: the top was Earth Inferno (later renamed Boneyard, though this didn't catch on), playing an eclectic mix of goth,

---

8   Non-autistic neurotype.
9   J Robb, *The Art of Darkness: The History of Goth*, Louder Than War Books, 2023

industrial, punk, post-punk, rock, psychobilly, 80s pop, and beyond; the middle was Wheels, consisting of rock, metal, grunge; and the ground floor, Shady Lady's (with a Saturday night club called Katch), played indie and pop. When I spoke to people about the space, there was confusion around what was named what, with many contradictory accounts. This feels fitting, as if the building resisted being pinned down by imposed nomenclature.

The entrance was towards the top of Victoria Street, through Nicky Tam's pub at 4 India Buildings, or the doors to the left which led us straight down to the sulphurous centre of the world. Built in 1864–66, India Buildings[10] were designed by architect David Cousin in the Scots Baronial and Jacobean style and came complete with bartizans, where I imagined a sentinel was stationed to keep us safe from violence before reaching our dark sanctuary.

The goth club suited its Old Town home with its cobbled streets, dark closes, the nearby High Street where the old Tolbooth prison once stood, The Hub's old church spire towering over Victoria Terrace, the grimy graffitied Cowgate with its gutters of puke and piss, and the old execution sites of the Grassmarket and Parliament Square (recently a filmset for Guillermo del Toro's take on *Frankenstein* by Mary Shelley, gothmother extraordinaire). And, fittingly, opposite the former entrance to Nicky Tam's is the Quaker Meeting House which stands on the spot that was once the home of the infamous seventeenth-century Wizard of West Bow, Thomas Weir, who supposedly dabbled in the dark arts.

10   Information on India Buildings and Victoria Street architecture from Historic Environment Scotland's Dictionary of Scottish Architects (scottisharchitects.org.uk) and Edinburgh World Heritage; India Buildings planning documents from the Edinburgh Council planning portal (and in-person at the Plan Store).

Victoria Street curves up from the valley that is the Grassmarket, providing a route to George IV Bridge. The quirky street was designed by Thomas Hamilton during his tenure as architect to the Edinburgh Improvement Commissioners (1827–34) and in recent years it's become a popular tourist destination. But in the 1990s it had character and was home to various shops I was sure had portals lurking in some dark corner, including the gloomy Polish shop selling ornaments and striking posters that felt like you'd walked into an Angela Carter novel. It was also home to another favourite haunt: Byzantium. Originally St John's Church and now a fish and chip restaurant, it comprised various bric-a-brac and antique stalls scattered throughout the vast space, with a dark (of course) cafe in the rooftop where you'd settle with cheap tea and biscuits as you admired the treasures you had found in the market below. Victoria Street thrilled me as a teen; it genuinely felt like a real-life fantasy bazaar and not the hollowed-out Instagram backdrop it's become.

It's clearly appropriate that a portal on this street provided merciful release from daily life for glamorous queer goth kids every Saturday night.

Shifting dimensions

Over the decades, the outer Old Town shell of 4 India Buildings has remained much the same aside from a few cosmetic alterations as it changed hands and purpose, but the interior morphed, disorienting people who were familiar with its previous incarnations. Even for those who frequented either The Rocking Horse or Espionage, many would imagine extra floors, recounting getting lost and losing friends, as if the building were a queer, living creature with shifting dimensions. It feels fitting that the interior is as bewildering as the outside layers of the Old

Town, and as the innards shift, the exterior is sure to quiver in response: the crowstepped gables rippling and threatening to collapse, machicolations adducting and abducting like fish gills as the startled pilasters' vermiculated banding sinks beneath the building's epidermis. The stonework settling, the banding expunged and reinstated, the disturbance is merely a transient blip in our periphery, our epistemic framework precluding our ability to fully witness the movements, leaving us with a nebulous unease.

The buildings still have the power to discombobulate, even from a distance. Trying to work out what became of the Earth Inferno space, I looked at the luxury hotel planning documents submitted between 2015 and 2024 for the combined premises of India Buildings, 11–15 Victoria Street and Cowgatehead Church – including the empty lot on the Cowgate where us clubbers were spat out every Sunday morning. Despite protests from local residents, the plans went ahead and Virgin Hotels opened in 2022. I'd originally thought the hotel, like some architectural body horror, had subsumed all of India Buildings, but gaps remain. It transpires that No.4 and its basement floor where Earth Inferno once existed, is 'outwith demise', which feels appropriate somehow, as if our queer dancing formed an invisible sigil, keeping Earth Inferno beyond the reach of the luxury hotel's encroachment, resisting the gentrified death of the surrounding buildings.

But is it empty? Who owns it? A Virgin Hotels staff member said it was bought to prevent the Espionage nightclub from operating and is used as storage, but other staff couldn't corroborate. Savills estate agents have a large sign blacking out the old window of Nicky Tam's telling us that on 4–15 Victoria Street, retail units are to let, over ground and basement. Work is being carried out on the old Nicky Tam's premises, so I assume it's been let and look it up on the planning portal. It's been snapped up, but the shop is siloed, with no access to the basements below; the stairs we once traversed down to Earth Inferno are greyed out, walled off. I can't find any planning applications for this basement level, but it's possible it's been let and it's simply suspended in an in-between state. I look again at the Virgin Hotels map, at the area 'outwith demise' that is the basement level which was once Earth Inferno, and I can see the shape of the club: the pillars in the middle of the dancefloor, the seating area behind the arches, the toilet reception area, the enclosed fire escape that was our exit onto the Cowgate after swaying to 'Venus in Furs' and hissing at the sudden bright overhead lights of the 3am closing.

It surprises me that I can still see its outline. I wonder if I'll recognise it if I get the chance to set foot in there again, I wonder if Savills or Virgin Hotels staff would indulge me and let me play the Sisters and have one last, eerie dance. And what of the other levels, where the rock and indie spaces used to be? Unless I missed them, no planning maps exist for these floors. While the simple explanation is they're 'outwith demise', I imagine the buildings above floating over a living, morphing darkness.

I'm researching and writing this piece during the winter holidays, a queer point in the year where time simultaneously stretches and contracts and the people I need to speak to are unavailable. I hover in this liminal time, waiting for staff to return to their workstations before I can (potentially) creep back into the infernal darkness of 4 India Buildings, decades after I last set foot on the premises.

No record
I booked an appointment at Edinburgh Council's Plan

Store,[11] spending a couple of hours fascinated by old planning maps spanning the 1960s, 1970s and 1980s. But the 1990s Rocking Horse era seems to be undocumented; there's nothing in the Plan Store, nothing online. I chase Savills staff about accessing the space, but when I manage to pin someone down, they tell me they don't have anything available in India Buildings and have no record of ever having a property up for rent on Victoria Street.

I'm writing this in one of the Virgin Hotels bars, ironically called The Commons Club (I appreciate the building is in use after years of neglect but can't help but think what a difference it would have made to the community if it truly was for the commons). Yesterday, Virgin Hotels staff took me on a superficial tour of the premises, giving me a feel for the sprawl of the building. The lovely staff member didn't know if the old goth club floor in the basement level of 4 India Buildings belongs to them and said they'd investigate. Given I couldn't see the Earth Inferno space itself, I asked to see the room directly above, currently a kitchen and restaurant, and with a nod to The Sisters I can now say I walked on the ceiling of Earth Inferno. As I did so, I pondered the mysterious space below, appreciating its stubborn reconditeness, the way it remains just out of reach.

I imagine getting access to the basement, walking down the stairs between coat check and dancefloor, and I can almost feel the glitch, the time-slippage, as I simultaneously experience past and present. While this piece must come to an end, the Earth Inferno space has lodged itself in my consciousness and it feels almost mythical. Is it

11   Thanks to Derek Struth at the Plan Store, and also Rebecca Carr and Lucy Cousins at Virgin Hotels.

even there? To paraphrase The Sisters: does it exist when it can't be seen? If I ever get to traverse those basement stairs, will it flicker into being?

'The self that is at odds with everything around it'

I was reborn on Victoria Street.

Like a (scruffy, tattered) phoenix in the cleansing flames of Earth Inferno, sure, but officially in 2 India Buildings next door, where the Registrars Office was based (it's also where James and Julia got hitched, as well as where my much-loved and much-missed sister Rachel got married).

I'd been using the name Ever off and on amongst friends since I was thirteen. In my late teens I decided to officially claim it, and in my early 20s I picked up a new birth certificate from the Victoria Street registrars.

Born again. Praise be.

This wasn't the reason for the new name, but I like that Ever is gender neutral. I call myself a woman, but mainly because I generally fail at mainstream idea(l)s of what a woman is and I like to pervert that, but I don't care if someone calls me she/her, he/him, they/their, creature, monster, or whatever else. I have no real attachment to any gender, which I guess means I'm genderfluid or gender-queer, but I've never felt a need to name it. I realise what a privilege that is, that I can't ever be misgendered, that I don't need to fight for gender-affirming healthcare; I feel for my fellow queers who are trans or non-binary in a hostile country where bigotry has been stirred up by the press and certain people in positions of power. I can't help but be reminded of existing as a queer person in the 1990s under Section 28, which prohibited local councils from 'promoting homosexuality', supposedly because simply by existing as themselves, queer children were (according to Thatcher) 'being cheated of a sound start in life'. But like the current removal of healthcare for trans young people, it was a bigoted, damaging legislation that denied students proper sex education, fostered an acceptance of homophobic bullying and ruined the lives of many children and young people.[12]

I'd spent my youth being moulded by other people, carrying a name imposed on me when I was a small blob of a thing. It feels absurd this is a norm; surely choosing your own name makes sense (which can of course include the decision to keep the potentially temporary name gifted when you emerged screaming). I was empowered holding my shiny new birth certificate. It was approval from authorities, but I was no longer defined by other people; I was writing my own narrative. A dangerous move, because people don't like when you step out of the box they've fixed you in; they attempt to constrain you and arrest your processes, the myriad of becomings that you were and are and will be. In response to me asserting myself by choosing my own name, my relatives said I was 'in darkness'. I'm reminded of author Osamu Dazai: 'Try to move an inch and the blood comes spurting out' (it did), and the Japanese proverb: 'A nail that sticks out will be hammered down' (they tried).[13]

But my body and soul are nobody's business but my own and I am ever and always skinkleglam in darkness, cut through by strobing lights. Let down by bigoted legislation and my Procrustean bio family, I found a home amongst freaks and weirdos in Earth Inferno, but what home can today's trans kids find in a country that tells them they can't know themselves, that sets them up as

12   BBC, 'Section 28: What was it and how did it affect LGBT+ people?', 1 November 2019, www.bbc.co.uk/bbcthree/article/cacc0b40-c3a4-473b-86cc-11863c0b3f30, accessed 26 March 2025

13   O Dazai, 'Cherries' in *Self Portraits*, New York: New Directions, 2024 (translated by Ralph McCarthy)

scapegoats and strips them of bodily autonomy? We have a duty to support all queer kids. In the 1990s, Earth Inferno was a safe space for people of various genders and sexuality. In the 2020s, the whole country should be a safe space for queer people.

My queerness isn't only sexuality or gender. The illustrious Black queer feminist bell hooks described queer as 'the self that is at odds with everything around it and that has to invent and create and find a place to speak and to thrive and to live'.[14] It's a way of seeing, of engaging with the world, slantwise, sklentin, embracing the strange, odd, peculiar, bizarre, weird, unconventional, unorthodox, uncanny, unexpected, unfamiliar, abnormal, anomalous, out of the ordinary, extraordinary, mystifying, perplexing, deviant, aberrant, eerie, unnatural, creepy, spooky, freaky. I'm grateful for those formative years in Earth Inferno, where my queerness was consolidated, and now, in middle-age, forever eldritch, I traverse Edinburgh's streets, seeking and creating queer portals.

14   bell hooks, 'Are You Still a Slave? Liberating the Black Female Body', The New School, 2017 (available on YouTube)

Mary's Cottage

LEWIS HETHERINGTON

Mary's Cottage started life as the coach house for the big fancy house next door. It sits on the west side of Loch Goil, just outside Lochgoilhead. A beautiful but unfussy stone building, painted white with blue dormer windows poking out the front and back, nestled into the rolling landscape of Argyll. Holding steady as time and people drift through.

There I am in the back garden. All limbs and tie dye t-shirts and friendship bracelets I made for myself. There I am with my sisters. We scramble over the lichen covered stone wall, following the sort-of path that stumbles down the hill to the loch. Clumsy bodies, hot with sun. At the shore there's a boat. There's always a boat, from somewhere. We bundle in and push ourselves out into the gentle waves. Rowing as best we can. Looking at the rocks and seaweed softly glowing under the water below us.

There I am in the back garden, my sisters are inside with their own secrets. I'm alone, a streak of a boy with tufty sandy hair, poking around in the garden, peeling moss off rocks.

There's a glass conservatory at the back of the house. Boxy and simple. There I am, just outside it, poking at a broken bird. Sometimes the birds don't see the glass and they crash into the window and fall, left to die on the paving slabs. I'm looking with creeping horror at this lifeless thing, soft feathers on its underbelly.

How did the bird not see the window? How can it be fair that life can create invisible walls for us to crash into?

My big sister makes a poster that says STOP BIRDS!!! It has a drawing of a bird in flight inside a red circle with a line across it. She puts it up with Blu Tack in the middle of the pane that they tended to crash into. It works. The birds don't crash into the glass anymore. It took me a while to work out that the birds weren't actually reading the sign. But still. They saw it, and it made them realise that something was there. Stopped them crashing into that invisible wall.

*

'Mary was formidable.'

That's what my mum says when I ask her.

'She was just an incredible woman.'

I remember Mary being tall, with a wiry, dynamic frame. She had straight grey hair, serious-looking glasses dominating her face, but a bright glint in her eye. I have a tendency to romanticise everything but my mum stresses how special she was.

'She went back to work after having children, back when no one did that. There was no maternity leave back then. At all. Her husband looked after the kids. She was just so tenacious.'

She worked as a research scientist at the Buildings Research Establishment (BRE) in East Kilbride with my grandad. The organisation was founded in 1921 to provide 'homes fit for heroes'. There was a desire to rebuild after the First World War in a way that raised living standards[1]

---

1   BRE Group, 'The history of BRE', bregroup.com/about/history/timeline, accessed 2 April 2025

– a nationalised effort to create better places for people to live in. The organisation was privatised in 1997, no longer a place of national investment, but a place of profit.

My grandparents moved to East Kilbride not long after the BRE office opened in 1949, to rebuild their life after the Second World War. They had been living with my grandad's parents in Edinburgh. They were enticed by the gleaming concrete visions of a New Town with good jobs, community, culture. My mum recalls at that time it was jokingly called 'Nappy Valley' because of all the young families flocking there. That's where they met and became friends with Mary, and she told them about her cottage in Lochgoilhead, which they could use whenever they wanted.

On arrival you had to note down the meter readings in pencil, in a lined notebook on a little wooden table under the stairs. It was a history of the many and varied guests. You could leaf through the thin pages and find our trips from years gone by. You'd note the meter readings again on leaving so you could pay for the electricity you used. And you'd be expected to do something for the upkeep of the place; clean the gutters, paint a wall, fix a fence. My mum remembers one time the water coming into the house was a funny colour, so they went up to the burn that supplied the cottage and found a dead sheep in there. They had to hoick it out to get the clear water flowing again. Mum can't remember what they did with the dead sheep.

I think about what it means to make a place. The Buildings Research Establishment testing materials for durability and warmth. The bold clean futuristic lines of East Kilbride. An old coach house turned into a cottage with crumbling stone walls. What are the structures we make for ourselves and for others? Do they make us happy?

The cottage always felt alive. Alive with the breath of people and nature flowing through it.

*

There I am floating through the walls and floors and up and down the stairs. My mind often takes me to Mary's in my dreams. What part of me is still there? Am I a ghost, haunting that place, refusing to let go?

*

My mum recalls the journey she would make as a child with her family, travelling to Lochgoilhead from East Kilbride. They had no car, so it would be the train to Glasgow, then a train to Arrochar, then a bus. They got the steamer sometimes, which went all the way to the Lochgoilhead Pier. Their trunks were always sent ahead, waiting for them at the cottage. As she talks she realises memories are blurring into each other of all her different visits. She remembers people lined up on the pier, waiting for the visitors to arrive. It was a tourist destination then, but nothing like now.

At that time, the farmer next door offered to sell Mary a field next to the cottage for £10. She wasn't remotely interested. The same amount of land now would cost about £200,000. These days the sloping hills that surround the loch are lined with identikit caravans and holiday homes.

When I ask my Mum what she did at the cottage when she was young she says, 'Same as you when you were little. Just run about exploring, seeing what was new, what strange and interesting things we could find, playing the purple piano.'

*

There I am in the back room. Bashing out notes on that purple piano, still there, somehow lodged into the wall. It's a ramshackle machine that seems to have assembled itself from scraps of wood and metal gathered nearby.

There I am, studiously coaxing something like music from it. The keys are smooth like polished bone, but you never know what sound you'll get. Some of the hammers are stuck together so you get two notes at once, or sometimes it's an empty thud, or sometimes it's like a honky tonk from a saloon bar in a cartoon, or sometimes it's a resonate bong that sounds like it's emanating from deep below the earth's surface.

The rest of that room was a chaotic miscellany of outlandish treasure. A shark's jaw. A giant conch shell with gleaming iridescent insides. Endless old books. Was there a model plane? Possibly. Battered leather chairs? Almost certainly. I'd make dens there. Woollen blankets smelling like earth that made me invisible. A silent cave boy happy and snug away from the world.

*

We'd go to the cottage a few times a year. Easter holidays, summer holidays. Half term break from school. From the mid 1980s to the mid 1990s. We had moved from Newcastle to Shropshire when I was four, and again to Yorkshire after that. My young life had a not unhappy sense of transience, but the pilgrimage to Mary's Cottage was a constant.

First off, we'd drive to East Kilbride to stay a night or two at Granny's house. We'd go to Victor's and I'd get battered black pudding and chips. We'd visit the concrete elephants in the park. We named them Salt, Pepa and Spinderella, in homage to the band. I loved these elephants. I would pet them, let my whole weight flop on their sturdy backs. They were stoic and still, suspended in mid step. I willed them to move. I willed them to uproot from the ground and take me far from everything. They didn't move. They couldn't offer me that. But still, I had Mary's Cottage.

*

Other people knew before I did; that my boy-ness was not correct. That the type of boy I was, which was, and is, the only way of being a boy that I know, was wrong. That somehow that boy-ness, which to me was as natural as breath, was somehow, to others, awkward or even shameful.

I remember running in the playground at school. Screaming and wild as we charged at each other in a game of Bulldogs. Tackling each other to the ground. I remember playing rounders, the sun hanging high in the sky, we'd hold our breath as a ball got thwacked up towards the edge of space. We'd run like our lives depended on it. I remember when we played football, barely forming teams or playing actual games. Just legs running, a ball rolling, and our tiny voices screaming with delight.

But somewhere along the way, it became apparent that I was not doing things right. One late afternoon, the golden sunlight fading, we were all on the back football pitch behind the primary school. The girls had been slowly phased out of our games. The sound was no longer tiny voices screaming with delight, but frustrated dads barking out instructions which I didn't understand. Football morphed from a giddy mess of flailing limbs to this uneasy arena where masculinity was scrutinised. I did not know how to play by these new rules. The other boys seemed to know innately what to shout, how to posture, how to perform 'a boy playing football'. Dads would shout angrily at our failures; I didn't know how to correct them. They were perfectly nice dads I'm sure, unquestioningly performing the roles they were expected to play to maintain the social structures they had accepted as life.

The game was nearing its end. I made some mistake and the exasperated groans made my inside flip. All of a sudden I didn't know how to be. Like a bird hitting a pane of glass. Flitting through the air and crashing into an invisible wall.

*

One weekend the newspaper came with this special kit for keeping track of the football league tables. It was a huge cardboard contraption, with lots of little slots all over it, so you could monitor where all the football teams were in the rankings. The names of all the teams came on little brightly coloured tabs of cardboard. As games were won and lost you were supposed to move the tabs up and down accordingly into the appropriate slots. I would at stare at it, studiously, uncomprehendingly, desperate for it to reveal its secrets, to give me the knowledge that would make me fit. Or at the very least let me know how to fake it.

Around the same time, it was becoming apparent that being friends with girls wasn't just being friends with girls but it was *being friends with girls*. I remember that my girl friends would come round and dress up as Take That to perform 'Relight My Fire' in the back garden. I cast myself as Lulu and, in a wig and a dress, I would leap, spectacularly, out of the raspberry bushes. It was a pocket of joy, but I understood this was something to keep confined within the walls of my own back garden.

Increasingly I knew that my behaviour, my voice, my hand gestures were all ... something. Something to be commented on. Something to be noticed. Other children and parents and teachers, and sometimes just people on the street, showed me, by the way they looked at me, that my way of being a boy was wrong. And when that would happen I'd get a hot tingle of shame surging through me. I was crashing into invisible walls all over the place.

It was the final year of primary school, and a boy, let's call him Andrew Bowman, who ranked highly in the social order of things, said that no one was to be friends with me anymore. If anyone wanted to stay friends with him, they were not to talk to me again.

He was just another little boy, following the rules of the structures that had been shown to him, trying to feel happy, trying to feel safe.

*

There I am at the top of the hill on my bike. Sometimes at Mary's Cottage we would get money to go and buy sweets. Me, my two sisters, and whatever other kids were about. There were always other kids about, the Fishers from over the road, or sometimes family friends who had come to stay. We'd grab our bikes and go jangling off down the road. After a few minutes we'd get to the top of the hill and pause, readying ourselves for the descent.

There I am at the top, looking across to the far side of the water, the shop in the distance beyond the loch. After a moment of suspension I freewheel down the hill. Soaring. Blues and greens flashing before me. The air lifting me up.

*

There I am, creeping out of bed, along the wooden floorboards of the upstairs landing in the middle of the night. The adults are up late, talking and drinking wine by the fire. There I am peeking through the gaps in the floorboards below, with my sisters as partners in this daring escapade. We're watching the faces below, flushed from drink and the fire, becoming these new adult creatures, not parents but something else.

Mary's Cottage was all about in-between spaces. Where things could change. Where you felt inside and outside at the same time. It was a house that almost didn't seem to know what a house was supposed to be: gaps in floorboards, rattling windows, a giant trunk in the living room full of nothing but wooden clogs, moose antlers above the fire (how the moose antlers got to this cottage in Argyll is one of the house's many mysteries), noisy creaking steps, clocks that didn't work. A shapeshifting space of comfortable strangeness. A softly glowing home for anyone who visited. Set in a garden of half grass and half bog, jewel tones of green and blue in the sparkling sunlight. The boundaries between everything seemed thinner there. The veils between worlds. The possibilities.

*

At school I was learning to shrink. To not inhabit my body the way it wanted to be inhabited. I didn't know what was acceptable and what wasn't, so shrinking felt like the safest option.

When did those words creep in, *gay-boy, poof,* and all the others? I don't remember where they came from but they appeared, sharp, heavy and lurking in the air. Others knew those words were for me before I did. What was I supposed to do? Was I to gravely and solemnly accept these labels, keep shrinking and try to cause as little offence as possible? Or was I supposed to angrily reject them, prove I was a real boy? And if so, how did I do that?

I didn't know.

Who was I meant to be?

*

At Mary's Cottage my body was just my body. A creature, an animal, a breathing thing.

*

Years later now, and I am outside Mary's Cottage again. I have been walking the Cowal Way with my sisters and my boyfriend. A 57 mile trek from Portavadie to Inveruglas (though we only went as far as Arrochar in the end).

It's coming towards the end of day three of our trip, the sun is bright, and we're tired but happy. We are walking down into Lochgoilhead from Curra Lochain. The sight of many childhood swims. We have a hotel booked, but of course we planned to have a little stop at Mary's Cottage.

But it's not Mary's Cottage now. She sold it years ago. We don't really know anyone in the village so we had planned to come here and ... then what? Stand here in reverence?

However. The day before, we were in Strachur and we went for a pint with Pam Fisher who used to live over the road from Mary's Cottage. It was her kids who would often be part of our intrepid childhood adventures while she would chat by the fire with my mum. We mentioned our planned pilgrimage to the cottage and she said, 'Oh the new owner is lovely, you should just knock on the door.'

We couldn't believe it.

But that's what we did.

There was a moment of puzzling, as he looks at these dishevelled hikers on his doorstep, my sisters, my boyfriend and me, patchily telling a story about family holidays and Mary and a purple piano and a chest of wooden clogs. And then something, possibly our earnestness, prompts him to throw open the door and welcome us in.

The layout is unchanged. We enter through the old flimsy porch at the side of the house and into the wee kitchen. Tea is poured, beers in green bottles emerge from the fridge. One of my sisters asks how he came to buy this place. Turns out, he also stayed at the house on holiday as a kid, his family had a connection to Mary too. When she came to sell it, he just knew he had to take it on, take on the stewardship of the place. Keep it alive and breathing. We find warmth through the fragile connection we have to each other through this building.

I ask to use the bathroom and he starts to tell me to go through the living room and up the stairs – and he stops with a moment of recognition because I, of course, know where to go. I know every step of this house. I walk into the living room and the scale of it still feels massive. It contains a vastness of memory and meaning that expands beyond the dimensions of its wood-panelled walls.

The house is filled with a new miscellany of treasure. Posters and memorabilia and mementos from things that he loves, projects he has worked on; he's even installed a cinema screen in the back room. I go upstairs and resist the urge to wander along the corridor to the bedroom at the end of the hall. There's no need to snoop around, because Mary's Cottage still exists, exactly as it was, nestled in the folds of the landscape of my memory.

I go into the bathroom; it hasn't really changed. I look at the bath wedged under the sloping eaves and I can feel the scalding hot water washing away the mud from my legs, many years ago. I wash my hands and press the little plastic soap dispenser shaped like R2D2 from Star Wars. It makes his signature sound of frenetic yet cheerful squeals and bleeps. I head back out to the landing.

And there I am. A streak of a boy with tufty sandy blonde hair. A ghost holding onto that place. I look at him. I am proud of him and the friendship bracelets he made for himself, of his open heart and clumsy limbs. We look at each other and I tell him he doesn't need to worry about what kind of boy he is. He is who he is. He takes a moment to consider this and then something shifts, his furrowed brow softens and that sad little ghost boy is released. He melts happily into the air.

I head downstairs. With my sisters and boyfriend I continue the hike; we need to get to our hotel for the night. We follow the same route which we used to ride on our bikes. With tired bodies we trundle down the hill, and I feel light as air.

Piper's Cave

RONA MUNRO

Piper's Cave is at Keil, near the southernmost tip of the Mull of Kintyre in Argyll. It's a narrow cave hollowed out by ancient, higher, sea levels, which now sits at the base of a cliff of grey and pink tinged rock, a few metres from the narrow road and shore beyond. It is one of the three Keil caves, the other two labelled as 'The Great Cave' and 'The Hermit's Retreat'.

The caves were not labelled with formal signage when I was a four year old, five year old, eight, eleven or fourteen year old, scrambling around their seabird salty interiors, absorbed in my intense and solitary 'pretend games' (even at fourteen ...). The foreshore and the area around the caves show signs of human habitation from Neolithic times. The caves were probably regularly used for shelter and habitation over the centuries; a nineteenth-century census reports that Keil Cave was home to at least two families in 1881.

When I was a child, the caves were inhabited only by seabirds and jackdaws and full of the musty smell and black grapeshot debris of sheltering sheep.

I knew their stories though. Or, very specifically, I knew the legend attached to Piper's Cave, a narrow, triangular hole in the hillside, its farthest end high enough for a child to stand up in ... stand and stare into the darkness that seemed to extend even farther through an opening too small for any human. A cold air seemed to blow from it, as if there were some larger, unseen cavern beyond.

It was to the legend of Piper's Cave that I returned when I wrote a really rough, early play, struggling to make a character who spoke some of my experience. They were a character who fell in a messy place between understood gender identities. I did not have the insight or a contemporary sense of cultural permission to understand that this was what I was describing, back then. When I read that play now, I see that at times I spelt out what I was doing in as many words, but I didn't, entirely, understand what I was trying to say. At the other end of my life I might understand better, now.

The story describes a certain kind of man and a supernatural intervention that destroyed him. In my retelling I was trying to evoke the place that swallowed him up. And I was trying to create a character in opposition to him, one struggling for alliance with the things that terrified him, the natural world, the unnatural, supernatural creatures of myth. In my early childhood, the Mull of Kintyre was not a pipe band pop song, it was the wild tip of a peninsula of soft fertile farmland, and, for me, that was what it always evoked.

It was a place where I felt I had rested between things, sky and sea, outer and inner worlds, concrete and floating identities. The use I made of the story of Piper's Cave was well to one side of its original meaning, but ... bear with me.

This is the story – there was a piper, well known in Keil. His name was Alisdair and he played at every dance and ceilidh or gathering at that end of Kintyre. He was the best piper anyone had ever heard. He went everywhere with his little terrier dog; they were inseparable and the wee dog would sit at his feet as he played for the dancing.

So Alisdair was at a ceilidh, a wedding or just a party sprung up on a night the work had gone well and finished early and there was ale to hand. And probably a fair bit of ale had been taken for, picking up his pipes and wiping the sweat from his face before he started again, Alisdair called out, 'Now I'll give you a tune as good as any that's played by the wee folk themselves in their cave there by the shore.'

And everyone went quiet because, in his pride, Alisdair had done a very dangerous thing: he'd claimed he could outplay the musicians of the fey, the sìthichean, the Kindly Folk who lived inside the hollow hill and, it was said, danced their nights away in the great caverns there, in fairyland. You must call them the Kindly Folk because they're always listening, and, as their gaze is often on the damage and destruction mortal creatures have made in the beautiful world we share with them, they are quick to take offence.

Claiming you might play the pipes better than their best was definitely likely to cause offence.

So one of the folk dancing there, maybe it was a farmer whose land lay alongside Alisdair's little croft, maybe it was a woman who had loved him since he was a bairn, spoke up, worried and warning him. 'You can't say that, Alisdair, that should not be heard.'

But he was full of ale and the joy of his power to make any creature dance and his huge and happy pride. He doubled down on that boast. 'I wager you that I could walk into the cave at Keil Point, I bet I could travel all the way through the hill, playing my pipes, I promise I can march through all the caverns of those fey folk and I'll charm them so well they wouldn't dare harm me. That's how good I am.'

(I felt, then and now, that as a representation of a certain kind of pride, the kind usually culturally assumed to be the property of men, this takes some beating.

Just because it was said it didn't mean he had to do it, but this sort of pride can never, ever, back down.)

So, the whole gathering walked with him down to Keil, they all gathered behind Alisdair as he paused at the black entrance to the cave. In those days – the story said – a dark path led all the way into the hill ... but no one had ever dared walk in there.

There were plenty in the watching crowd still urging Alisdair to turn back. At his heels his little dog was shivering, tail clamped between its hind legs, eyes fixed on the dark cave in clear terror. But Alisdair was bold and defiant as he shouldered his pipes, waking the instrument with blasts of breath and then struck a rousing reel and strode away into the cave. And, frightened but loyal, his little terrier dog followed him into the dark.

And for a long time the crowd still heard the reel, growing fainter and fainter as Alisdair walked further into whatever lay inside the hill ... and then there was a terrible sound, the squawk of bagpipes dropped and flattened, the air screeching out in discord. And then they heard high unearthly keening, eldritch shouts of rage ... and then they heard howling, terrible howling. Alisdair's wee dog burst out of the cave, its little eyes starting from its head. All the fur had been singed from its back and it was yowling in terror. Behind the terrier the roof of the cave collapsed with a rumble to leave only a tiny opening. No one could ever walk into the hillside again, even if they dared.

The people waited at the cave mouth for a long time. But no one ever saw Alisdair the piper again.

However, if you put your ear to the ground on the

green hill above the cave, they say you can hear him, still playing his pipes and lamenting his imprisonment in the land of the fey for all eternity.

That was the story.

I knew it was basically impossible. For one thing, as the daughter of a geologist, I knew this was definitely a cave eroded by the sea long ago. It wouldn't really extend further than any high tide had ever swept into it, certainly not into the underground caverns of the Kindly Folk.
I knew it was fantasy.
I absolutely believed it.
And its meaning, for me, was that the places between things, without certainties, were real and potent and should not be forgotten.
Like the little dog who loved too much, this truth terrified me, but it attracted me far more.
I also believed that it was perfectly possible for a human to also be a seal, and, as I was told the name Rona means 'seal woman', I believed when they talked to each other – raising their whiskered snouts out the waves at Keil Point and calling mournfully to each other – they were calling to me too. (You'd think I'd be better at swimming in that case.) The sound of their singing made me cry, as if reminding me of something I'd lost.

I believed that place, that landscape, was mine. I believed I understood it, its legends and its forgotten power, in ways that were invisible to others. I believed this of all the wild landscapes I inhabited, at home in North East Scotland and on holiday in Kintyre. In those places I had a strong, secret, identity. They were called Jimmy.
When we lived in town, whenever I was sent to the

corner shop for messages, I became Jimmy as soon as I left the house. In that shop they believed that was who I was, a wee boy called Jimmy who came for butter and sugar and eggs. I loved going to the shop.

But even then Jimmy was never male in the way I understood that gender role from popular and familial culture. Jimmy was, for me, something more potent and ambiguous than that. They were strange and wary and watchful, completely who I craved to be, completely hidden from view unless I was running over the field or edging through the woods trying to move as silently as a fox.

Once we moved out to the countryside, a very large part of my time, the time not claimed by school or by voracious reading, was spent outside making my own paths through small feral worlds – woods, fields, burns and burrows.

If you had seen me then, you'd have seen me crawling under the broom bush where I'd made my den, talking earnestly to the beech tree I'd named and believed had a dryad female soul and was my one true love. You'd have seen me lying under the larch trees sheltering from rain showers, watching bullfinches hopping above me. In my hand would probably have been a sharpened stick. I was very fond of the persona of a historical warrior, probably modelled on some character from books by Rosemary Sutcliff or Geoffrey Trease.

I can date this time of lying in bushes, bows and arrows, and fantasising dryad love by the landscape I claimed, that I inhabited every second I wasn't at home or in school. I was ten when we moved out to rural Deeside; I've found drawings of my beech tree true love in old school papers and jotters from second year of secondary school, so I would have been thirteen. I'm fairly certain that this imaginative life and identity continued beyond that into my fourteenth year … which was why it was so deadly deadly secret to the point that even now I feel nervous recording this. I had a fantasy … no, another world in which I was someone other than my school persona. I had no vocabulary for what I felt like in that world. I felt like myself, authentically, completely, myself. But that self was like no version of a teenage girl I had ever encountered. And I was a teenage girl, in the 'real' world, there was no escaping that 'certainty'. The person I was in the woods had to be a private relief, a secret, a pretend game.

Kids' stuff.

When did I stop being Jimmy?

Around the time I kissed a boy for the first time I suppose. But the cause and effect is not clear. It was very clear to me that I'd hit the age at which I ought to kiss a boy and I had always been very competitively determined to hit every one of life's milestones as soon as I could. I was aware that kissing a girl was also an option but it was not one that carried the same status and it didn't present itself. In any case, this was not about desire. At this point, and for some time, I don't think I actually experienced genuine desire for anyone. Enjoying the kiss wasn't important. It didn't factor at all. The goal was to get kissed (of course nice girls didn't initiate) and success was measured by whether the boy expressed any desire to ever do it again.

From that point on, in certain areas of my life I lived in a place of confused, powerless, self loathing and misery for many years. But I didn't forget being Jimmy. I just buried them even deeper inside, but they were alive.

*

Piper's Cave is a play I wrote about ten years later. I'm glad to say it would be extremely hard for anyone to track down a copy. It was not good. It is not terrible, and it means very well, but it is almost completely devoid of humour, and has a static plot that repeats and repeats to the point where, on re-reading, I could have happily erased all the play's characters, especially the one who miserably and long windedly represented my own experience.

This character is called Jo. They are trekking through a version of the landscape beyond Keil Point on the Mull of Kintyre. In my early 20s I spent several days walking and camping in that landscape alone, apart from my dog. I kept a diary of each wild day. A lot of those observations of seals and seabirds and huge lonely skies and sea are replicated in the play. Those are the best bits. A record of a person sinking into communion with place, whose identity is just the physical experience of each moment of bog and burn and stinging wind.

> *'I was up the hill. I slept up the hill under the sky, burrowed into the bracken and when I woke up it was morning. I was looking down on the clouds, they were sweeping round the sides of the hill and I was above them in the sunshine … Couldn't believe they were just water vapour, the wind and the sun were boiling up weather from the sea to sweep inland. They looked alive. They were moving like animals, water and air, moving and mixing and changing into something else … I walked until dark and then I heard the seals singing …'*

We learn that, before the action of the play begins, Jo suffered an assault, an attack by a stranger on the street. A man chased them/her into the stairwell of a tenement and held her/them prisoner for several hours. The man told them they might be killed. The man told Jo that he had just assaulted his own girlfriend and now had no reason not to continue the violence. Jo escaped this situation by talking and talking and listening and listening, calming their assailant, promising they heard him, promising him he wasn't a monster and could be understood, extending empathy to save their own life. In the end the man is relaxed enough to slacken his grip and Jo is able to escape.

This was my own experience; I wrote the story of my assault exactly as it had happened, with one change. In the play the man marks Jo with a knife. I was unscarred, visibly.

This was not the only time in my life I would be seriously or sexually assaulted but it was the first. I was nineteen.

In the play, Jo is crazy in love with another woman, but clearly it is unrequited and Jo is extremely confused as to the nature of their/her desire.

Again, this was based on my own feelings, but I was even more confused than Jo. One thing I had in common with the character, however, was a determination to assert that there was no connection between being assaulted by a man and feeling desire for a woman. There was no cause and effect. That might seem an obvious thing to assert these days, but those were different times.

I relocated the cave of my childhood to the wildest, loneliest point of the Mull of Kintyre. There, in the middle of wilderness, Jo stumbles into Piper's Cave and finds it already occupied by a fellow traveller, a wild man, a tortured soul called, obviously, Alisdair. He is a contemporary man but also the piper of the story trapped inside his own terror and by the hubris of his acts of arrogance and destruction.

Jo is a person he sees as female, as obligated to extend comfort and empathy, as an appropriate target for his rage if she refuses to do so, as the blame bucket for all the fear and loss in his life. As someone required to save him.

What I was trying, struggling, to express was the real injury I felt after being attacked. It was not a literal sexual assault, I was not raped on this occasion. I did think I was going to die.

> *'I was walking home on a Saturday night. It was about eleven o'clock. I was just passing the cinema when this guy fell into step beside me, ranting. I couldn't make out what he was saying, just those breathless, violent words coming out in a spray of saliva. He had mad poppy eyes. He was quite young ... I said go away ... I said go away and I started walking faster and ... oh fuck he was following me, so I started to run, I was yelling for someone to help me, anyone ... but the Saturday night crowds just parted to let me run through them with him at my heels ... I got to the street door onto our stair and he slammed into it right behind me ... I couldn't hold the door ... he got in.'*

I was pinned down by my throat for hours on the tenement stair and threatened with strangulation over and over. It was a situation I talked myself out of. I used every part of me to strain to connect to this guy, to make him see me as human, to sympathise with him in the hope he would sympathise with me.

It worked. After hours of talking, of listening, to his pain he let go of my throat. He let me shift away from him, just enough, that I was able to jump up and run. And though he lunged after me I was fast enough to get away and put my flat door between us.

I didn't go to the police. It didn't even occur to me. I felt completely complicit in my own destruction. To survive I had had to forgive him, to live I had to feel that forgiveness, to mean it so sincerely that he could not doubt me. I felt dirty and ruined and the worth of my love and empathy felt soiled forever. I was so ashamed.

But it was worse than that. Part of who I was felt annihilated, because what he'd seen, what had made me a target for his violent attention, was fuck all to do with who I'd thought I was. Seeing myself through my attacker's eyes I was just a frail, young, solitary creature with a particular body shape, legitimate prey.

That person, the one he attacked, was not the woodland warrior, the lithe feral creature of the forests and fields, was not Jimmy, or anything like them. Jimmy was violently exposed as a figment of my hopeful imagination.

It was a forceful rebuke to my presumptuous ambition to any other identity than the one he had targeted. A rebuke that was reinforced by almost everything else around me. How stupid was I to secretly shelter another idea of myself, worse, how shameful, how dishonest.

This attack came at a young moment when all sorts of exciting and passionate and seemingly contradictory desires were boiling up in me. That could, I think, have led to many different places. But the attack felt like fate's punishment. I experienced it as a violent instruction to close all that down.

Clearly, I didn't, not entirely. In *Piper's Cave* desirable contradictions still struggle for clumsy life.

In the play, in my rewriting of the legend of Piper's Cave, Jo and Alisdair are both trapped in the cave, in a place between things, in a supernatural world and in a landscape which is constantly in flux, constantly transforming, refusing certainties. Both of them are terrified but over the course of the play Jo finds a way to let herself be absorbed into this world without fear, to defeat her terror and allow herself to simply be, a potential, an identity of infinite possibilities.

As described, *Piper's Cave* was based on some of my actual experience, my many identity confusions, the attack I was still processing years after it occurred, and my life-long visits to the Mull of Kintyre. A lot of its detail was largely lifted directly from the diaries I kept in those days. I still have those diaries and I re-read them before writing this piece.

And what a boggy mess of misery and self loathing I uncovered. They made for very difficult reading. I understood why the play was such a confused and complicated creature, a beast that didn't understand its own shape – neither did I. What I read on those pages were the thought processes of a young person desperate for certainty, in all things, but especially in their idea of their gender identity and relationship choices. What I read were the thoughts of someone who was completely failing to find certainty and absolutely hating and punishing themselves for that failure.

But, within that, was another voice, one which whispered as loud as it dared, 'Why do we need to be certain? Why are we afraid to live in a place between things?'

> '*Black roaring night ... and me lost in the middle of it ... But it was beautiful, you know? Every so often there'd be a break in the rain and the moon would flash through the clouds and I'd see the whole hill, everything bent double in the wind that was screaming round my head and all the burns turned to avalanches of water and foam, boiling up and trying to eat me alive ... I thought it would be the end of me but I loved it.*'

Piper's Cave is a flawed play about a loved place that still, like sunlight breaking through on a hillside, has flashes of a beauty that move me yet. And I am proud of the fleeting moments in which I managed to stand up for the liberation of utter uncertainty, to be a human whose identity cannot be bound by labels or expectations or appearance or relationship choices, a creature undefined by their damage or desire, a fluid being.

> '*You've got furry fingers Jo. Furry fingers and toes. I've seen them. You've got teeth Jo. And claws. You're a little monster. You lie under the bathwater and stare at the ceiling and practise breathing through gills ... You've cat's eyes and ears and great she bear arms to hug me till the bones crack and you sneak out of bed at night to prowl along the roof and howl at the moon.*'

When I revisited *Piper's Cave* I revisited the memory of that assault. I hadn't, as I believed, properly processed its effect, likely I never will, entirely. But I also revisited an assertion of fluid identity that I tried to make, that slipped away from me, ignored again as the confusion of my life and the failings of the play itself consigned 'Piper's Cave' to a drawer. I rediscovered, for all its faults, a play that still kept something beautiful and hopeful alive.

It took me a long time to claim 'they' as one of my pronouns. I felt I was appropriating something only permissible to those forty years younger than me. I did it, am doing it, quietly, stealthily, edging that part of my truth out into the open – a nervous half step at a time.

Younger people I work with now probably do not know what it means every time they matter of factly grant me the pronoun 'they'. Every time it is a little shock of happiness, sharp enough to bring tears to my eyes. I didn't know how strongly I would experience that until it happened. It's one of the things that gave me the courage to look back into Piper's Cave.

I always identified with the little dog in the story of Piper's Cave, not because they followed a destructive man but because they loved as I often did – fiercely, helplessly loyal, but so misguided, certain they knew the right destination but utterly clueless. They were so damaged by where their love took them. But they survived. They went into terrifying uncertainty and chaos but they escaped when the piper could not. And afterwards, maybe, they had a wilder life. Somewhere, out there, they're surviving yet, fierce and safe and living their old dogged life between land and sky and all the world's wild and changing things.

Or maybe they're not a dog any more, maybe they've decided to become a seal.

'It's dark. Dark and warm. I'm floating. I'm floating in salt water. I'm breathing without lungs, without gills … I'm hanging, hanging in the dark. I am sleek.

I am silver. Raise a whiskered muzzle out of the water, roll in disguised as a ripple, sing in a voice that makes you cry ... as though reminding you of something you've lost ... Sleek and silver. Hanging in the dark, waiting ... waiting ... That's all.'

who will be remembered here

The Project

This project – *who will be remembered here* – was conceived of and led by playwright Lewis Hetherington (he/him) and visual artist CJ Mahony (they/them), working in partnership with Historic Environment Scotland.

The result has been a series of films, and this book. Where this book explores places which aren't necessarily considered historically important but are significant to real life queer experience, the films respond to sites of established historic significance. We wanted to make visible the lives that have been rendered invisible by the way our history has been presented to us.

For the films, we collaborated with four queer writers – Robert Softly Gale, Harry Josephine Giles, Robbie MacLeòid and Bea Webster – working in BSL, English, Gaelic and Scots. They responded to beautiful and striking sites and environments across Scotland, asking questions about the stories we choose to tell and how those stories shape the lives of those who come after us.

who will be remembered here is an archive for the future, capturing the lives of queer bodies and ensuring their stories carry forward.

Visit **www.fieldworkperformance.co.uk** for details of how to watch the films.

Acknowledgements

Our heartfelt thanks to all of the writers who have contributed to this publication.

We are grateful for your candour and for your honesty.

To all of those at Historic Environment Scotland who have supported the project, specifically Alasdair Burns, Neil Gregory, Gillian MacNee, Karen Scrymgeour, Catriona Morrison and Robbie MacLeòid for their support in making this book happen. We want to offer special acknowledgement to Christine Wilson for her rigorous, thoughtful and sensitive support as we pulled this book together.

Thanks also to Mairi Sutherland for proofreading the text.

Thanks to Matt Addicott and Susannah Armitage for offering insight, guidance, ideas and a friendly ear as required.

Our love and thanks to Georgie Grace and Iain Craig. Ceud mìle taing. Tha gaol againn oirbh.

Image Credits

The Library is a Queer Thing
Woodside Library, Aberdeen
Emma Murphy

The Strathclyde Suite
Plan of Bothwellhaugh Roman Fort and bathhouse
HES SC353653

Red Blaes and Blue Moon
Glen Kinglas and the 'Arrochar Alps'
HES DP193219

Sm:)e for 2004 / Sm:)e airson 2004
Stage door and light store, Cumbernauld Theatre
HES DP230439

A Subtractive Process
Detail of *Objects Dream* by CJ Mahony
Rob Hill

My Sapphic City
Map of High Street from *The Early Views and Maps
of Edinburgh 1544–1852*
HES SC495600

The Club, 4 Queens Crescent
West Princes Street and Queens Crescent central garden
HES DP219387

20-Something Spittal Street
Spittal Street Clinic, Edinburgh

Little Gless Box
Amusement arcade coin pusher machine
David Gee / Alamy Stock Photo

Nowhere
Inverness High School, 1985
HES SC1825006

Glasgow's Queer Foundations
The Strand Bar, Hope Street, Glasgow, 1971
HES SC2541876

Earth Inferno
India Buildings, Victoria Street
HES DP404060

Mary's Cottage
Lochgoilhead, Argyll
Anne Hetherington

Piper's Cave
'The Great Cave' and 'Piper's Cave', Keil, Argyll
HES SC1330426

Authors

Damian Barr is an award-winning writer and broadcaster. His memoir, *Maggie & Me*, won Stonewall Writer of the Year and *Sunday Times* Memoir of the Year – in 2024 he helped turn it into a play with the National Theatre of Scotland. He hosts series for Radio 4 and the BBC's *Big Scottish Book Club*. His new novel is *The Two Roberts*, fictionalising two queer Scottish artists Robert MacBryde and Robert Colquhoun. Damian holds a PhD in Creative Writing and is a Fellow of the Royal Society of Literature and the Royal Society of Edinburgh.

MJ Deans is an actor and reluctant writer from Cumbernauld. She is a fluent Gaelic speaker and has a 1st Class Honours degree in Acting from Motherwell College (now New College Lanarkshire). When she's not acting and writing, you can normally find her with a crochet hook or game controller in her hand, or hiding out in the cinema watching anything involving vampires or superheroes.

Mae Diansangu is a queer poet and spoken word artist from Aberdeen. She has performed at literary festivals across Scotland and appeared on BBC Scotland's *Big Scottish Book Club* and BBC Radio 4's *Tongue and Talk*. Her series of poems 'black lives, heavy truths' is part of the National Library of Scotland's collection. Her debut collection, *Bloodsongs*, was published in 2024.

Ashley Douglas is a multi-lingual historian, writer, translator and consultant, specialising in the Scots language and LGBTQ+ history. She has worked with and written for a range of national heritage and literary organisations, including the National Library of Scotland, Historic Environment Scotland, the Scottish National Portrait Gallery and the British Library. She recently consulted on *Katherine: James V*, the latest instalment in Rona Munro's *The James Plays* series. Her first full-length book, a historical biography of Marie Maitland, will be published in 2026.

Ever Dundas is a queercrip shapeshifter. Their monstrous amorphous selves can be found lurking in or near Edinburgh portals. They're cofounder of the Inklusion Guide: 'a kickass guide to making literature events accessible for disabled people' and author of critically acclaimed novels *Goblin* and *HellSans*. They are currently working on a novel that is one big love letter to music.

Ink Asher Hemp is a poet and multidisciplinary artist based in Edinburgh. They write, sometimes on their own and other times in community, but always for care informed by climate justice, queerness and disability justice. It's time to build tomorrow through the stories we tell ourselves today because the future is fiction till we breathe it.

Lewis Hetherington is a playwright whose work is rooted in collaboration and storytelling. He often works with community groups and young people to amplify unheard voices. He has written for National Theatre Scotland, Edinburgh International Festival, Citizens and Lyceum Theatres amongst others. His work has won two Fringe First Awards and an Adelaide Fringe Award and toured all over the world.

As a writer, **Johnny McKnight** has had over 60 professional theatre productions staged, including the award-winning *Wendy Hoose*, *The Joke* and *A Perfect Stroke*. Johnny has been described as the 'vanguard of post-modernist panto', with over 30 original commissions. He also has over 50 hours of screen credits and was nominated for the Royal Television Society Scotland Best Writer 2023, with his anniversary episode of *River City* winning Best Drama 2023. He is currently under commission to develop two musicals, a sitcom and a feature film.

CJ Mahony is a visual artist whose practice spans sculpture, installation and writing. They've undertaken projects in the public realm for Tate, Opera North, ITV, National Theatre Scotland, National Trust and the Contemporary Art Society. CJ works as an independent mentor and has tutored and lectured for institutions including Glasgow School of Art, Norwich School of Art and the University of Cambridge.

Jeff Meek is a lecturer in Economic and Social History at the University of Glasgow. Jeff has published widely on LGBTQ+ history, including the books *Queer Voices in Post-War Scotland: Male Homosexuality, Religion and Society* and *Queer Trades: Male Prostitution and the War on Homosexuality in Interwar Scotland*. Moving to Glasgow in 1989 from rural Galloway Jeff threw himself headfirst into the queer scene, before giving university a try in 2001. Jeff maintains the website www.queerscotland.com.

Rona Munro has written extensively for stage, radio, film and television. Her theatre credits include *The James Plays*, a cycle of multi-award winning contemporary plays about Scotland's history, the Tony-nominated *My Name is Lucy Barton,* adapted from the novel by Elizabeth Strout, and *Iron,* for which she won the John Whiting Award. Her television credits include the BAFTA-nominated *Bumping the Odds*, and her films include Silver Bear winner *Ladybird Ladybird* directed by Ken Loach. She is one half of The Msfits, a feminist comedy and theatre company whose other half is actress Fiona Knowles.

Ali Smith was born in Inverness in 1962. She is the author of several novels and short story collections including *The Accidental, Hotel World, How to Be Both* and the Seasonal Quartet. She has been four times shortlisted for the Booker Prize, has won the Goldsmiths Prize, Orwell Prize, Costa Best Novel Award and the Women's Prize. Ali Smith lives in Cambridge. Her latest novel, *Gliff,* was published by Hamish Hamilton in 2024.

Amanda Thomson is an artist and writer whose work is about our connections to the natural environment. She has exhibited nationally and internationally and her writing is in several anthologies. She is a regular contributor to *The Guardian*'s Country Diary. Her books include *A Scots Dictionary of Nature* and *Belonging: Natural Histories of Place, Identity and Home,* shortlisted for the Wainwright Prize for Nature Writing in 2023. *Boundary Layers*, a film-essay about nature's reclamation of the former Ravenscraig steelworks, was part of Scotland's exhibition in the 2023 Venice Architecture Biennale.

Louise Welsh is the author of ten novels including *The Cutting Room* and *To the Dogs*. Louise has a ten-year practice in opera with composer Stuart MacRae. She is co-creator/presenter (with Jude Barber) of the podcast *Who Owns the Clyde?* Louise is Professor of Creative Writing at the University of Glasgow, a Fellow of the Royal Society of Edinburgh and the Royal Society of Literature. She lives in Glasgow with her partner Zoë Strachan.

Historic
Environment Scotland

HISTORIC   ÀRAINNEACHD
ENVIRONMENT   EACHDRAIDHEIL
SCOTLAND   ALBA

We are the lead public body for Scotland's historic
environment: a charity dedicated to the advancement
of heritage, culture, education and environmental
protection. Through our books we are telling the
stories of Scotland – exploring ideas and starting
conversations about the past, present and future of
our nation's history and heritage.